Listening to What the Man Sang

The Casual Fan's Guide to Appreciating Paul McCartney

David Styburski

For MBA

Contents

Introduction

As far as musical acts are concerned, the Beatles might be the perfect necessary distraction during a global pandemic. Many years after a childhood obsession, I threw myself back into Fab-Four fandom within the long limbo of COVID-19, in part because so much of what they produced still exudes positive energy and because—when solo ventures are added to the group endeavors—there's more than enough to keep you busy over extended phases of lockdown.

I relistened to album after album in the background at home during the workday and closed each night by doing a similar deep dive into Beatles-related literature. The major books tower impressively in number over the albums, starting with Michael Braun's 1964 on-tour piece *Love Me Do!*, then on to a 1968 authorized biography (still an essential time capsule) by Hunter Davies, and all the way to Craig Brown's *150 Glimpses of the Beatles* from 2020. Many more in the middle of that chronological spectrum remain unchecked on my list of bedtime reading, along with new volumes coming out on a steady basis.

Going book by book reveals not only the gradual addition of supposed facts to the Beatles story but also—and more interestingly—important shifts in how the narrative and its main players have been framed.

The depictions of Paul McCartney have changed most consequentially in my view and have made a different hard-to-shake first impression on fans depending on when they initially heard his most famous works. In her revelatory analysis *The Beatles and the Historians*, Erin Torkelson Weber divides the biographies and other influential writings into four eras, each of which built and/or strengthened a distinct mythology: the Fab Four narrative (prior to the band's breakup), the *Lennon Remembers*[1] narrative (from breakup until John Lennon's murder in 1980), the *Shout!*[2] narrative (immediately post-Lennon to roughly the early 1990s) and, most recently, the Lewisohn[3] narrative. And although Weber's interest isn't focused specifically on Paul, you can track public and critical perceptions of him by each of those eras.

While with the Beatles, Paul was seen as the cutest and most accessible member. Upon their split, he came closest of the four to being vilified. Then, with the shock of John's death, the natural inclination to

---

[1] *Lennon Remembers* is a book-length interview with John by *Rolling Stone* magazine founder Jann Wenner in which Paul is essentially blamed for the Beatles' irreparable problems.

[2] *Shout!*, by Philip Norman, was the first major Beatles book published after John's death and is Lennon-centric in its summations.

[3] Mark Lewisohn is supposedly the world's only full-time Beatles historian. His books, particularly *Tune In*, work hard not to divide responsibility for the group's success unevenly among the four members.

amplify the deceased's contributions to the world resulted in even further dismissal of Paul's influence (as was also the case for the talents of lead guitarist George Harrison and drummer Ringo Starr). For John to be believed posthumously as a genius, it became useful—consciously or otherwise—to paint Paul as a wimp and his output as ineffectual.

Paul has spent the past 30 years—what Weber considers the Lewisohn period—attempting to regain control of his cultural stature and artistic credibility. He told his side of the Beatles' tale over 600-plus pages in 1997's *Many Years From Now,* took a victory lap for his songwriting and in-studio contributions to the Beatles' records in the just-released Hulu docuseries *McCartney 3, 2, 1* and has championed his classic songs proudly via constant touring.

That careful branding, though, has focused primarily on his accomplishments from the 1960s. The otherwise satisfying *Many Years From Now* doesn't cut into his solo years. *McCartney 3, 2, 1*, released just a day prior to the writing of this introduction, spends three hours with Paul while only addressing four songs written after 1970 (and none within the past 40 years). At the typical concert, he'll do 2/3 Beatles stuff and just 1/3 solo material, including nothing (minus the 1982 tribute to John, "Here Today") from 1977 to 2005. Those odd choices mean there remains so much more for new or casual fans to discover, much of which sold well upon release and can't exactly be categorized as obscure.

McCartney-centered projects not sanctioned by Paul have lacked comprehensiveness in other ways. Tom Doyle's *Man on the Run* book is an excellent chronicle of Paul in the 1970s but goes no further. Howard Sounes's *Fab: An Intimate Life of Paul McCartney* and Philip Norman's *Paul McCartney: The Life*, while hefty in page count, have "life" in their subtitles for a reason and tell straightforward chronological stories without pausing much to marvel at the music. So many of us have loved the Beatles for so long that we might forget—and need to be reminded—that their lives wouldn't be of interest if we hadn't fallen first and foremost for their songs.

I compiled this book with that previous sentence especially in mind. It's not a definitive biography and might admittedly not contain even a single new fact for die-hard fans. Consider it, instead, an invitation to pull out your vinyl or pull up your favored streaming service and listen along to each featured song in context. Particularly for the "casual fan" mentioned in the title, my ultimate hope is that it'll highlight both the major events and noteworthy tracks of Paul's career simultaneously. If you're more than intrigued by the end, here's wishing you'll go even further. Keep sampling the rest of his catalog and consider the thoughts/research of the authors, podcasters and critics mentioned in the Sources section.

Books and music aside, 2020 was also an opportunity for me to observe and benefit from a surge in Beatles-themed podcasts. I became aware of Weber's work through her appearances on the gold-standard program *Something About the Beatles* by Robert Rodriguez (formerly with Richard Buskin). Ireland's Jason Carty and Steven Cockcroft mix factual expertise with easygoing chemistry to make their *Nothing Is Real* show the most comfortable of listens. *Fabcast*, by Howie Edelson and Stephen Bard, conveys the kinds of passion and irreverence that can only come from die-hards who want every new piece of art to be great and aren't afraid to hold heroes to high standards. Each episode of Ethan Alexanian's *Fans on the Run* exudes an equal sense of fun and community. And there are many more.

The podcast world, in contrast to books, seems willing to treat Paul's later career with some seriousness. It's just as common to download the latest episode and hear a conversation about the merits of Paul's 1980s material vs. a back-and-forth on his songs from the Beatles' *Sgt. Pepper*. Even in debates concerning John and Paul and who holds more responsibility for the breakup, negative opinions about Paul's actions (or John's, for that matter) don't overwhelm the participants' appraisals of his musicianship. I've opted—maybe for the first time in McCartney texts—to treat those podcast discussions as a significant source of opinion and perspective for the book. To me, the assessments made in them are no less valid than those from the twenty-something and teenage writers in the early days of rock magazines. An informed perspective, on paper or on iTunes, is an informed perspective.

An extra-special mention is warranted for the *Take It Away* podcast, hosted by Chris Mercer and Ryan Brady. In addition to chronicling all of Paul's recorded output, the show was, in some ways, a meditation on what it means to be a fan. Does the true fan attempt to hold the artist accountable by judging new work against what he/she proved capable of producing in the past? Or is the best kind of fan someone with enough positivity and open-mindedness to always find hints of greatness where the less dedicated follower can't see it?

As I listened, Ryan drove me nuts because he seemed to absolutely love every single item in Paul's discography. But it was such a treat to hear his first reaction to an unearthed rare entry in the McCartney songbook. "What is THIS?!?" he'd pose with infectious glee to his friend Chris.

Ryan died suddenly in a car accident a week after I began typing away on this book. He studied music at Northwestern University, where he attended one of Chris's classes and realized that his teacher loved the same unreleased Wings song ("Cage") as him. ("Wait, YOU'VE heard this song?!") He wound up working as a marketing exec in Los Angeles for Atlantic Records.

I never met the guy but interacted with him briefly online and received a kind reply. We'd likely attended the same convention for Beatles fans at some point without my knowledge and where there was allegedly a secret room with all the bootlegs you could ever want to purchase. Had we connected back then, Ryan would've likely been suave enough to have known the password for entry and good-hearted enough to have shared it with a near-stranger who gave him a hard time for liking the second side of Paul's *Red Rose Speedway*. Whatever your thoughts end up being in regard to this collection of words, you can either blame or praise Ryan's memory for indirectly giving me the idea.

"Coming Up" (Studio Version)

(Paul McCartney)

Artist: Paul McCartney

Year of Recording: 1979[4]

Appears on: *McCartney II*, *All the Best* (non-US version)*, Wingspan (Hits and History)* (non-US version), *Pure McCartney*[5]

It's mid-1980, and a retired John Lennon is surfing stations on a car radio in Long Island, New York, with his personal assistant behind the wheel. He's hyper-critical of what he hears, switching channels after no more than a minute and proclaiming how he could've done such and such a song way better than the artist performing it. He turns the dial yet again, makes a

---

[4] Due to differences in release dates by country, recording dates are being used to introduce each song instead. For officially released material by Paul after the Beatles, Luca Perasi's exhaustive *Paul McCartney: Recording Sessions* is the main source. For dates related to Beatles material, see Mark Lewisohn's game-changing work in *The Beatles: Recording Sessions*. Tracks not found in either of those sources were referenced against the online database www.the-paulmccartney-project.com.
[5] Discographies in this text are intended to be instructive, not comprehensive. Many out-of-print and/or special editions of albums have been excluded for the sake of readability.

quizzical face and shouts, "Fuck a pig! It's Paul![6]" He lets the song finish, gets home and soon orders the same assistant back on the road for two items: A stereo system for his bedroom and a copy of "Coming Up."

John listens to the song nonstop for days, and it drives him "crackers" until he finally picks up a guitar and writes a mea-culpa tune ("I Don't Wanna Face It") based on Paul's riff. Two months later, he's back at work after a five-year break, armed with a bunch of new songs and ready to make the comeback record— and the last creative output of his lifetime—*Double Fantasy* with wife Yoko Ono.

And what, I wonder, was John so afraid to "face" in his response to his ex-bandmate? Might it have been the realization that they were indeed at their best as partners and that life was too short to let their bond die? If John wants "a friend [he] can rely on" or "peace and understanding," Paul suggests he sit tight. Coming up!

Bored by his work with the post-Beatles band Wings, Paul seemed ready for a come-to-Jesus sort of change at this time, with a restlessness not entirely unlike

---

[6] John's initial reaction to "Coming Up" was documented by personal assistant Frederic Seaman in the memoir *The Last Days of John Lennon.* A late-career insider of the Lennons, Seaman faced legal challenges from Yoko Ono for possessing John's diaries. His book and Robert Rosen's *Nowhere Man* provide competing views on John's last years.

John's. Earlier that year, Wings had pulled every string imaginable to finally book an expensive tour in Japan, where they'd been effectively banned due to previous drug busts. So, what does Paul do in early 1980 after such painstaking effort and preparation? He flies into the country with a half-pound of marijuana barely concealed under the shirts in his luggage and ends up serving nine days in jail for what could've been a seven-year sentence.

But Paul is no dummy and probably wouldn't have consciously done anything so stupid. Perhaps, even he has suggested[7], it was a subconscious act of self-sabotage meant to blow up his existing band and give himself the license to start again with arguably the only other musician he truly respected, if only that man could be roused out of semi-seclusion in America. After the bust, Paul let Wings die and played all the instruments on "Coming Up" himself, biding time until the next chapter[8]. If only they could "get together," Paul muses. Coming up!

Close to when John poked his head out again, Ringo Starr started preparing a new album of his own. There

---

[7] In the documentary *Wingspan,* Paul tells his daughter Mary, "It's almost as if I *wanted* to get busted."
[8] Although an in-concert performance of "Coming Up" became more popular in the United States, John's private and public comments about the song suggest that he'd mainly listened to the one-man-band studio version.

had been a series of internal feuds among the ex-Beatles in the decade since their breakup: John vs. Paul, Paul vs. lead guitarist George Harrison, John vs. George. Yet they all adored Ringo, the lovable and light-hearted but sincere diplomat who was just as unifying for their music via his steady drums. John penned a song way out of Ringo's vocal range ("Nobody Told Me") around this time but planned to record it with him anyway. Did John know, right before his death, that Paul had committed to being in town for Ringo, too? After years of alternating between cheap shots and teases of a reunion in the press, were John and Paul finally feeling just nostalgic enough to take at least one step forward together without viewing the proposition as a silly step back?

They'd speak for the last time on the evening of John's 40th birthday, not even two months away from his murder. "Do they play me against you the way they play you against me?" John asked regarding the supposed Lennon-McCartney feud during the Beatles' solo years. Paul confirmed it, and they hung up on friendly terms[9].

---

[9] The timing and quotes of John and Paul's last interaction come from Tom Doyle's careful and not catty *Man on the Run*.

Whatever Paul was expecting around the time of "Coming Up," he sure was confident about it, even claiming within the song to "feel it in [his] bones.[10]"

"Maybe I'm Amazed" (Studio Version)

(Paul McCartney)

Artist: Paul McCartney

Year of Recording: 1970

Appears on: *McCartney, All the Best* (some non-US versions), *Wingspan (Hits and History), Pure McCartney*

October 1969: It's been two months since John Lennon told the other Beatles privately that he wanted "a divorce," and Paul is starting to think the occasionally flaky John actually meant it. McCartney has fallen into the deepest depression of his life while secluding himself in a three-room, Scottish farmhouse with his wife, his children, an electric generator and no hot water. He's unshaven. He's drinking at all hours. He's grieving the loss of the band that mattered more to him than anything he can think of. And he's been uncharacteristically out of the public eye for so long that photojournalists from *Life* magazine have been

---

[10] For more speculation on "Coming Up," listen to the "Early 1980" episode of *Fabcast.*

assigned to investigate some college-campus conspiracy rumors about him being dead.

When the reporters finally track him down at the farm, Paul yells at them to leave. When they keep at him, he throws a bucket of slop in their direction, only to have the dousing captured by one of the cameras, and lands a punch to the shoulder. Thinking twice about the PR problem now on his hands, he gets in his car, catches up with the trespassers and offers them an interview in exchange for the incriminating film. When the story hits newsstands, it appears under the headline "Paul Is Still With Us."

But just how close were we from that not being the case? "Maybe I'm Amazed" was finished in the weeks after the farmhouse incident, and it's a song not only of love but about being rescued from darkness. Otherwise the eternal optimist, Paul often talks about it reverently, as if it came during a period of severe mental illness that might've gone very differently if not for his then nearly new spouse, Linda Eastman. Following a 1960s reputation as a charming but unfaithful playboy, he'd spend every night with her for the next 29 years minus the aforementioned nine-day Japanese jailtime. And he still sings it at most concerts as a tribute to her, long after losing the vocal dexterity to do it justice. Despite including it as the obvious centerpiece of his first solo album, he wouldn't release it as a single, maybe because it was too personal, too vulnerable and too much of a gift meant for her rather than something to milk for commercial consumption.

A more famous live version finally became a hit in 1976, but I prefer the original. As in "Coming Up," Paul plays all the instruments here, including a guitar solo that feels both extemporaneously raw and carefully perfect.

It's also largely the version used in the end credits of the episode "Lisa the Vegetarian" from *The Simpsons,* on which the couple made a cameo in exchange for the animal-rights message in the storyline[11]. "If you play the words to 'Maybe I'm Amazed' backwards," Paul assures Lisa, "you can hear the recipe for a really ripping lentil soup!" Indeed, if you reverse the take used on the television show, the ingredients are in there, along with Paul's cheeky declaration, "Oh, by the way, I'm alive."

---

[11] *The Simpsons* famously doesn't bother with much narrative continuity from episode to episode, but Lisa has remained "veggie" ever since as a condition of Paul's participation.

"Only Mama Knows"

(Paul McCartney)

Artist: Paul McCartney

Year of Recording: 2004 and 2007

Appears on: *Memory Almost Full, Pure McCartney*

By the time Mary McCartney chose to seek treatment for the lump in her breast, it was already too late. The cancer had spread, and she died within hours of being admitted to a hospital. Fourteen-year-old Paul was spooked by the bloodstains on his mother's sheets during his one visit there but otherwise had no idea it would be the last time he'd see her.

Mary made a lot more as a nurse than his father, Jim, did as a cotton salesman, and when Paul was told of her death, the nervous boy couldn't think of anything immediate to say except, "What will we do without her money?" He'd beat himself up over the remark for decades.

Whereas Beatle authors have been quick to psychoanalyze the impact of Julia Lennon's death on the son she left behind, comparatively little has been explored about the consequences of Paul's similar experience at an even younger age. In John's case, it was an openly bleeding wound to his self-worth for seemingly the rest of his life and explained, some would argue, his complicated relationship with his own children, his attraction to a subservient marriage with a powerful woman like Yoko Ono, and several songs in which he wailed against abandonment. Paul, though, has been less open about his own loss, other than the uncharacteristically personal reference to "Mother Mary" coming to him in a dream in the first lines of "Let It Be."

We know his mother's death was followed, likely not coincidentally, by his obsession with the guitar. He'd gotten a trumpet from his dad and traded it in for a Zenith acoustic model. Paul wanted to sing, after all, and you can't do much of that with a horn in your mouth.

We know he, like John, married a single mother who ultimately became a musical sidekick because he couldn't stomach being away from her for any significant duration. But we don't know much else about the specific long-term effects of growing up abruptly without Mary, maybe because his cheery public image has tricked us into thinking it wasn't such a huge deal.

Well, of course it was. And if the senior citizen who made "Only Mama Knows" is at all like anyone else who lost a parent during such early years, the mark probably still shows itself—consciously or otherwise—in ways that surprise him.

"Live and Let Die"

(Paul McCartney-Linda McCartney)

Artist: Wings

Year of Recording: 1972

Appears on: *Wings Greatest, All the Best, Wingspan (Hits and History), Pure McCartney*

Sean Connery is out, Roger Moore is in, and film producer Harry Saltzman is prepping to reboot his *James Bond* franchise. The series succeeds by delivering common tropes from one chapter to the next, not the least of which is a killer song for the opening credits.

On set for *Live and Let Die*, Saltzman is played the fully orchestrated version by Paul and Wings (the exact same one that would appear on record) and remarks, "That's a wonderful demo. Now, when are we going to make the real track, and who shall we get to sing it?[12]" He suggests Shirley Bassey or Thelma Houston. Former Beatles producer George Martin, who's been hired to coordinate the soundtrack and would always

---

[12] The website BeatlesBible.com includes a quote of Paul telling this story secondhand, although the same story minus the dialogue is also mentioned in several McCartney biographies. Author Luca Perasi claims Paul came to *Live and Let Die* after initially being offered a similar opportunity to write the title tune for 1971's Bond adventure *Diamonds Are Forever*.

be known as a gentleman's gentleman, somehow avoids doing a facepalm in front of the boss.

Many of Paul's solo songs up to this point gave credit to Linda as a co-writer. With most of the family's assets frozen temporarily by lawsuits related to the Beatles' demise, the shared authorship was assumed to be a crafty workaround for at least one member of the McCartney household to earn significant income. The music publishers who had to share royalties with her sniffed around, didn't buy it and took the couple to court for $1 million, insisting that Linda prove her ability to craft anything remotely musical[13]. Her contributions to other songs from this period are mainly undocumented, but Paul swears she wrote the reggae-influenced mid-section here.[14]

---

[13] Despite owning the Beatles songbook, Paul's music publishers at the time made most of their money in television. He settled the Linda matter by filming a one-hour special for their network.
[14] Not an incredible statement, particularly since Linda's first full song was another reggae number, "Seaside Woman," made in 1972 and put out under the pseudonym Suzy and the Red Stripes in 1977.

"The Lovers That Never Were" (Demo Version)

(Paul McCartney-Declan MacManus)

Artist: Paul McCartney and Elvis Costello

Year of Recording: 1988

Appears on: *Flowers in the Dirt (Archive Edition* only*)*

The problem with trying to collaborate with Paul McCartney is that he's PAUL MCCARTNEY. If you love the guy too much, your hero worship might paralyze your ability to offer constructive feedback. And if you dare strike a nerve with your criticism, there's a good chance you'll be reminded of his all-caps status defensively by the man himself.

Paul kept holding a torch for John Lennon long after his songwriting partner had died, seeming to expect the same spark with someone else and then retreating quickly when his preconceived standards couldn't be met. So, it was logical for his manager to push him into working with Elvis Costello. Like Lennon, Costello had roots in Paul's hometown of Liverpool. Like Lennon, he was a not-shy and sharp-tongued communicator. Like Lennon, someone who saw the world through glasses. Like Lennon, known at least slightly more as a lyricist than a composer. Like Lennon, a right-handed guitarist who could sit eyeball-to-eyeball across from the left-handed Paul and provide a nifty mirror image of the chords they played together.

The pairing worked splendidly from an artistic standpoint. There's an entire album's worth of demos that, until they got lost in the move from my father's house to my first apartment, were my most prized possessions and of which "The Lovers That Never Were" has been deemed widely as the best. If only they'd been able to finish them. If only—could it have happened?—they'd opted to tour as a duo.

Instead, they apparently clashed over what they wanted the final product to sound like. Elvis hoped for a sparse but tight production not unlike the Beatles' *Help!* or *Rubber Soul* albums. Paul, ready to be deemed "hip" again by late-1980s record buyers, was into Frankie Goes to Hollywood and Tears for Fears.

Most of the material was eventually sprinkled onto their respective solo releases over the next few years, albeit not in the exciting style in which it was conceived[15]. Everything finally came out in one package as part of a super-deluxe reissue of Paul's *Flowers in the Dirt*. For $200 a pop, the box set reunited me with my long-lost bootlegs and represents both the most ridiculous amount I've ever spent for recorded

---

[15] A cleaned-up and less urgent official version of "The Lovers That Never Were" appears on Paul's *Off the Ground* without any in-studio participation from Costello.

music and, dare I say it, something not too far from a bargain[16].

"My Brave Face"

(Paul McCartney-Declan MacManus)

Artist: Paul McCartney

Year of Recording: 1988

Appears on: *Flowers in the Dirt*

In several interviews, John Lennon would dismiss Paul as a great public-relations man. Indeed, Paul was the Beatle most likely to offer reporters a cup of tea and tell the same old stories in a way that made his listeners somehow feel like they were getting an intimate exclusive. But at least when it came to his standing in the biggest band in the world, it took him several decades to learn how to stick up for himself.

Immediately post-breakup, John moved aggressively to cement his version of the group's narrative by cozying up to *Rolling Stone* magazine and its founder/publisher Jann Wenner. The publication's semi-official stance was that Lennon was the Beatle who mattered, that Paul's music wasn't rock, and that anyone who was

---

[16] Quality aside, this expensive archival release is infamous among McCartney collectors because many tracks were made accessible to buyers only as digital downloads instead of physical product.

upset about the Beatles not being together anymore should blame McCartney for it[17]. Wenner would order his writers to redo positive reviews of McCartney's solo albums until their assessments got close enough to those principles[18]. After Lennon was murdered, Yoko Ono named Wenner as godfather to her son, Sean (a title that had been given to Elton John while her husband was still alive)[19]. Paul, meanwhile, attacked his former bandmate in code on his *Ram* album but was smacked down hard by John in response and spent the rest of the 1970s changing the subject whenever a Beatles-related question was posed.

---

[17] John helped give journalistic credibility to the magazine by granting it several early interviews. Wenner published one of them in book form as *Lennon Remembers* against John's wishes. It's raw, entertaining and full of unreliable hyperbole instead of facts. In other words, just what you'd expect from someone going through an emotional separation from a longtime friend/business partner. Subsequent books leaned on Wenner's interviews heavily when shaping their own version of the Beatles' story, often without providing context for John's comments.

[18] In Robert Draper's *Rolling Stone Magazine: The Uncensored History*, Langdon Winner, who was told to redo his take on Paul's first record, admittedly has since called the demanded rewrite "the sign of a good and strong editor."

[19] The close relationship between Wenner and Ono is detailed in Joe Hagan's *Sticky Fingers: The Life and Times of Jann Wenner and Rolling Stone Magazine*, a biography for which Wenner provided exclusive access.

Even after John died, Paul seemed uncomfortable asserting himself as an equal partner in the Lennon-McCartney story. The circumstances of the death (and the carefully coordinated Wenner/Ono response to it) elevated John's stature even more, and the first serious, independent Beatles biography (1981's *Shout!* by Philip Norman) added to the mythology for years by promoting the belief that three-quarters of the Beatles' collective talent belonged to Lennon[20]. Paul seethed privately but knew it was too soon to push back against John's posthumous image.

Then in 1988, two things happened. First, Mark Lewisohn's renowned *The Beatles: Recording Sessions* book chronicled each of the band's trips to Abbey Road Studios in minute detail and emphasized Paul's previously unknown contributions as a guitarist, drummer and general experimenter rather than just the pretty-voiced bassist. Next, at the insistence of Elvis Costello, Paul retrieved his classic violin-shaped Hofner bass from storage for nearly the first time since the '60s. The Hofner's comparatively thin sound requires more effort to translate well to disc, but it's an incredibility lightweight instrument, a great perk if its

---

[20] Norman refers to his "three-quarters" statement in the introduction to his own biography of Paul from 2016 and has admitted that his McCartney book can be read as a correction of that unfair analysis. For examples of how Norman's 1981 writings may have influenced the public's perception of Paul, see Erin Torkelson Weber's fascinating *The Beatles and the Historians*.

owner needs to sing and play for hours onstage. Despite some emotional unease with what his old toy had come to symbolize, Paul relented and plugged it in.

The first song recorded with the Hofner again (a Costello co-write) was not only unquestionably-Beatles-esque but self-assuredly proud of it. The guitar solo could've been from the same stretch as 1964's *A Hard Day's Night*, and the descending melody accompanying the simple line "take me to that place" is catnip for Lennon-McCartney enthusiasts[21].

Within a year, Paul would be back on tour for the first time in a decade. But whereas his previous stint on the road included just an obligatory four songs from the 1960s, the new concerts were nearly half Fab Four, half solo work. With a newly balanced reputation and armed with his old gear, he embraced being "Beatle Paul" again and has played the role comfortably ever since.

---

[21] Credit to Ryan Brady of the *Take It Away* podcast for this observation.

"Lonely Road"

(Paul McCartney)

Artist: Paul McCartney

Year of Recording: 2001

Appears on: *Driving Rain*

The *Driving Rain* album doesn't get much affection from McCartney fans, but I find it fascinating as a work of transition and a rare example of Paul not having much confidence in his instincts. Half of the songs are about losing Linda, half are about falling in love with his second (and ultimately former) wife, Heather Mills, and a good chunk of each reveals a man unsure of what to do with competing emotions of loss and rejuvenation: How can feelings for a deceased soulmate coexist with those for a new companion? How can people protect themselves without missing out on what they need? How soon after tragedy are we allowed to feel joy fully again without being suspicious of it?

Former New York Times music critic Allan Kozinn likely got it right when he questioned whether the album's lukewarm reputation has less to do with the music and more with people's negative opinion of

Mills[22]. Knowing what we know now, it's a document of somebody trusting his heart, taking a risk and (at least in some respects) getting burned. It's not at all what we music addicts want as part of our Beatles fix.

Paul's unsteadiness carried over to the album's marketing. On a collection that otherwise sounded surprisingly modern for its 2001 release date, he consulted with Ringo Starr of all people to pick the lead single, and radio programmers got stuck with the mawkish ballad "From a Lover to a Friend." Then 9/11 happened, and he pulled the nearly released record back and added the godawfully square "Freedom" as a hidden track[23]. Everything else on it might've been fresh, but those featured songs were the stale odors of an old fart.

Those factors helped bury tracks like "Lonely Road." After decades of criticism for writing about characters ("Eleanor Rigby," "Rocky Racoon," whoever "the man" is in "Listen to What the Man Said"), it's Paul, nearly at age 60, writing about himself and daring to be vulnerable with his audience. Listen to his vocal in the outro, and you'll hear an adult wailing in agony like a

---

[22] Kozinn's comments can be heard on episode #275 of the *Things We Said Today* podcast.

[23] In the wake of terrorist attacks on U.S. soil, "Freedom" risked being taken as supportive of Bush-era foreign policy in Iraq. Paul performed it on tour for a stretch but retired it to prevent misunderstandings.

terrified child. He's crying out for Linda not unlike John Lennon's pleading on "Mother" for his parents to come home. It's Paul taking up primal-scream psychotherapy 30 years after John put it down.

"Hey Jude"

(John Lennon-Paul McCartney)

Artist: The Beatles

Year of Recording: 1968

Appears on: *Hey Jude* (US only), *1967-1970, Past Masters: Volume 2, 1*

In 2020's *Bill and Ted Face the Music*, the movie's title characters are tasked with writing a song to unite the world. Back in 1968, all Paul McCartney wanted to do was let John Lennon's son and soon-to-be ex-wife know that he was still their friend and for young Julian, in particular, to understand that his parents' divorce wasn't at all the 5-year-old's fault. By the time John heard the tune, "Jules" had been changed to "Jude," and the other Beatle not only didn't have a clue about its origins; he was convinced that the lyrics were about him, Paul and Yoko. To *Playboy* magazine, John claimed, "The words 'go out and get her,' subconsciously he was saying, 'Go ahead, leave me.[24]'"

Wrong as it was, Lennon's interpretation probably softened him up and helped secure the song as the Beatles' first single on their own Apple label. (John, up to that point, had been campaigning hard for his "Revolution" as their next release.) For George Harrison, meanwhile, the "Hey Jude" sessions were perhaps the start of an irreparable rift. When George started answering every lyric with a guitar lick, Paul told him to knock it off in less than diplomatic terms, and the perceived putdown was never fully forgotten.

Paul didn't intend, either, for the track to go on as long as it did. He just improvised a few lines at the end, got caught up in the moment and couldn't stop for the next four minutes. The final version made it onto the radio anyway at over seven minutes and became their biggest hit yet.

I never responded to "Hey Jude" and considered it too hokey until I rewatched the promotional clip that played on various television programs, most notably David Frost's *Frost on Saturday*. Readers are strongly encouraged to do the same.

---

[24] John's *Playboy* interview is most famous for his track-by-track recounting of who—Paul or John—wrote which songs. Paul does the same in his authorized biography, *Many Years From Now*, written with Barry Miles.

The band's in-studio appearance with Frost is full of amusing little bits: There's Paul, five seconds in, about to ask for something from the crew, then realizing the live recording had started and sheepishly backing off. There's the band giving Frost a gently hard time by doing a short, tongue-in-cheek version of Elvis's "It's Now or Never." There's an adorable moment within the presented clip where Paul must've given John a goofy look for forgetting to harmonize with him[25].

More than anything, though, I love watching the crowd and its diversity during the "Nah, nah, nah" section, and I keep waiting for someone to interview all these people about their memories for a book. Who were they, and what became of them?

Old, young, white, black, native Englander, immigrant, flower child, nerd, etc., I doubt it was an entirely conscious choice, and yet it tells you everything you need to know about what has made the Beatles' popularity sustain for so long. Their music—never more obvious than in "Hey Jude"—is happy music, and it's for everyone ... including the mysterious, aging hippie around the 6:24 mark who eventually gets right

---

[25] The instrumental backing was pre-recorded for the clip, but the vocals were live.

up in Paul's face and was probably annoying the living hell out of him[26].

"Riding to Vanity Fair"

(Paul McCartney)

Artist: Paul McCartney

Year of Recording: 2004 and 2005

Appears on: *Chaos and Creation in the Backyard*

Paul's temper tends to present itself in passive-aggressive ways. When his parents made him mad as a child, he wouldn't pout but would sneak into their bedroom and make a small rip at the bottom of their curtains. Even if they eventually noticed, he was a good enough actor to blame it on his younger brother.

If Paul has hard feelings for any of his former romantic partners, he's largely disciplined at keeping it to himself. The tight-lipped peace between him and one-time fiancée Jane Asher is especially impressive, with 50-plus years having gone by without either one muttering an ugly public word about the other.

---

[26] I wrote the main text of this book prior to reading Craig Brown's *150 Glimpses of the Beatles*. In one chapter, Brown tracks down a few participants (non-actors) and even takes note of the same odd, groovy bloke near the song's end. But I'm still waiting for a full book. Go ahead, Craig. I dare you.

Even his post-divorce songs about Heather Mills ("Gratitude," for example, recorded around the time of their split and released later) take a mile-high road when all he really had to do as a gentleman was politely keep his mouth shut. Theirs was a tempestuous romance with a famous story about a sickly expensive engagement ring being heaved from a high-rise window and lesser-known anecdotes about Paul writing songs to pull her out of deep depressions or Paul waiting for a conciliatory callback after a sudden confrontation that didn't make sense to him. Following their wedding, rumors also arose about Heather's restlessness, as if she'd had an idea of what living with a Beatle would be like and was shocked by the lack of excitement[27].

Paul would be quick to praise Heather for saving him from the darkest phase of his life. Yet it seems fair to say she needed some kind of saving, too, albeit maybe from more complicated problems that he wasn't equipped to fix.

---

[27] The *Take It Away* podcast does, in my view, some of the fairest commentary on the Mills/McCartney marriage as part of its "Chaos and Creation in the Backyard" episode without relying on some of the more sensational headlines.

Whoever hurt Paul so badly in "Riding to Vanity Fair," he says it wasn't Heather[28]. The 19th century novel *Vanity Fair*, after all, is only about a young woman who manipulates others to snag a respectable marriage and financial security within high society. And the magazine with the same name, after all, is only the same publication to which Mills gave an interview a few weeks before they tied the knot. Or maybe the reference is to John Bunyan's *The Pilgrim's Progress* and its use of the term as a marketplace that attracts the most materialistic of shoppers.

No matter the origin, it's quietly the angriest Paul has ever been on record. Given his personal history and its lack of kissing and telling, we'll probably never know why[29].

---

[28] Some wonder if the target was Paul's longtime PR man Geoff Baker, whose employment ended abruptly after a bad night between Paul and some reporters.

[29] Halfway into the writing of this book, Paul released the song "Lavatory Lil" and admitted uncharacteristically that it was a takedown of a real person. Even then, he teased without naming names.

"Let It Be"

(John Lennon-Paul McCartney)

Artist: The Beatles

Year of Recording: 1969 and 1970

Appears on: *Let It Be, 1967-1970, Past Masters: Volume 2, 1*

When I was kid, I would cry at the last scene of the very solid full-length documentary *The Compleat Beatles* (great narration by Malcolm McDowell, now nearly impossible to see)[30]. John, Paul, George and Ringo do "Let It Be," and it would always make me so sad to know they'd broken up. Regardless of any music-related loss, I didn't understand the concept of them not wanting to be so close anymore. How could they not be friends forever? The idea of a shelf-life in relationships was lost on me and, for better or worse, often still is.

I'm a Paul fan because he's shown a similar attitude about his old group. Despite his complex role in pulling the Beatles apart, he was the one who took the separation the hardest and the one who didn't want to move on. If John in particular had shown any interest

---

[30] Rumor has it that Paul bought the rights to the film in order to take it off the market, eliminating the competition for the officially sanctioned *Beatles Anthology* project.

in reuniting for even a moment, we know Paul would've sprinted over immediately with his tail wagging[31].

When the surviving members finally regrouped in the 1990s to make *The Beatles Anthology* (documentary and tie-in CDs), it was partially because George Harrison—the most steadfast holdout—was having financial problems due to sour dealings with a former business partner. But in the outtakes filmed for television and shown later on DVD, you can tell Paul is on top of the world. He didn't care if it meant recording on George's terms (at George's house with George's favored producer, Jeff Lynne) or filling the non-studio time with jams on ukuleles (George's favorite instrument)[32]. He's so damn happy to be together, even as he falls back into the same overbearing behavior that pissed the others off in the '60s.

Getting out of George's car in one segment, Paul is trying SO hard to be nice to him, while at the same

---

[31] Paul turned down the chance to reunite with George and Ringo at the Concert for Bangladesh benefit in 1971 and was a no-show at the Beatles' induction into the Rock and Roll Hall of Fame in 1988. John had died by the time of the latter and refused to appear at the former unless Yoko Ono could perform too.

[32] The title was also a compromise. The project had been floating around since the early 1970s as *The Long and Winding Road*—after a Paul song—but got changed to *Anthology* in a bid for neutrality.

time acting so self-consciously like the unanointed leader of the pack. "Nice motor ... Nice motor ... Well ... Should we go in and make a record?!" Under his breath, George must've been muttering, "This *effing* guy..."

With their guitars out, Paul is trying SO hard to connect with George by playing the twangy instrumental "Raunchy," the same song George performed on a bus to John and Paul in 1957 as an audition for the Beatles. But then, Paul can't help himself and wants to keep going. "Can we do 'Blue Moon of Kentucky'?" An unsmiling George wants to leave, thinks, "This *effing* guy ..." again and relents. "Just a shortened version."

With enough footage shot for the day, Paul thanks George for his hospitality and doesn't get a response. Ringo, ever the peacemaker, bails them both out by saying, "I LOVE hanging out with you guys." Ringo knows to say it for the camera and for their legacy. But for Paul, probably more than a little too much, it's actually true.

"Best Love"

(Steve Martin)

Artist: Steve Martin and the Steep Canyon Rangers

Year of Recording: 2010?

Appears on: *Rare Bird Alert*

Saturday Night Live producer Lorne Michaels offered the Beatles a facetious $3,000 in 1976 to reunite on his show. "Split it any way you want to. If you wanna give Ringo less, that's up to you."

Paul and John saw the program at the latter's New York apartment and nearly hopped into a cab with the intention of crashing the broadcast as a gag.

Paul would eventually appear on *SNL* five times, which meant he'd inevitably cross paths with one of its classic hosts, Steve Martin. The idea of them collaborating on music might terrify their respective fan bases, who shouldn't be scolded for expecting a misguided, odd-couple one-off.

But wouldn't you know it, "Best Love" is one of the sweetest works involving late-career Paul and far from a goof. Like Martin's wonderful novella *Shopgirl*, it's gentle, compassionate, not the least bit fussy, and packs a ton of feeling into concise and simple language. The line that always gets me is the one about even thinking his girl's ex-boyfriend is great. What a selfless sentiment, and what a tribute to a partner's unshakable decency.

Paul was energized by his shared laugh with John over the *SNL* invitation and came knocking the next night, too, this time with a guitar in hand. John was exhausted that day and always less wired than Paul for trips down memory lane. "Please call before you come over," he told his excited visitor. "It's not 1956, and turning up at the door isn't the same anymore." The iciness thawed during long-distance phone calls from then on. But they'd never meet again[33].

"Wanderlust"

(Paul McCartney)

Artist: Paul McCartney

Year of Recording: 1980 and 1981

Appears on: *Tug of War, Pure McCartney*

Many believe—and far fewer care—that Paul was the world's most famous pothead[34]. But his inner choirboy

---

[33] Pieced together from Tom Doyle's work in *Man on the Run*. Beatles author and podcaster Robert Rodriguez points out that Paul has dismissed the *SNL* story after decades of going along with it but that John's detailed memory of the event plus documentation of Paul having been in town make the anecdote seem more than credible.

[34] Paul told Tom Doyle in 2007 that he'd quit.

keeps him from owning up to it in some cases, often to the point of eye-rolling ridiculousness. After a 1970s drug bust, he claimed to have received a mysterious bag of seeds in the mail, only planted them out of curiosity and had been shocked, SHOCKED at what grew.

"Yeah, well, we got a load of seeds, you know, kind of in the post," Paul explained to a television reporter. "And we didn't know what they were, you know, we kinda planted them all. And five of them came up illegal." Oh, those pesky seeds…

In 1977, Paul had a recording studio installed on a yacht and made an album there (literally "yacht rock"). He and family spent their free time on another boat, whose captain huffed but didn't puff when authorities and customs officials inspected the vessel on at least two occasions. The band was cited for making loud music after hours without anyone finding anything suspicious in the ashtrays. Still, the captain's nose wasn't fooled, and he gave his passengers some angrily stern lectures about the risks they were all taking. Paul responded to the killjoy by chartering another craft, the *Wanderlust*, where he'd be left to smoke in peace.

Part of me wishes the story behind "Wanderlust" involved more substance and not just substances. Divorced from its origins, it has several passages of melodic beauty and could inspire those who long for a more permanent escape or rescue than what's possible in a quick toke. Paul has never played it to an audience but seemed to acknowledge its specialness by recording two versions within just a few years of each other, first for his *Tug of War* album and second for the soundtrack to the film *Give My Regards to Broad Street*.

Paul even earmarked the tune as a possible semi-Beatles reunion by asking George Harrison to add a guitar solo to the midsection[35]. When Harrison didn't show, Paul got a hold of the group's producer, George Martin, and had him insert a horn section instead.

"Tug of War"

(Paul McCartney)

Artist: Paul McCartney

Year of Recording: 1980 and 1981

Appears on: *Tug of War, Wingspan (Hits and History)*

Less than six months after John Lennon's death, Yoko Ono gave an interview to Beatles biographer Philip Norman and said that Paul "had hurt John more than any other person." Stunned and concerned about what she might've meant, Paul phoned Norman at home and asked for the context behind the remark but never had his call returned. Norman rationalized that he'd already written everything he could about the band and

---

[35] Paul and Linda appeared on George's 1981 tribute to John, "All Those Years Ago," around the same time.

didn't see the point in giving Paul McCartney a ring to help him understand more about his recently murdered friend[36].

Paul ultimately ranted to another journalist and confidante, Hunter Davies, about the situation and assumed (wrongly) that his uncharacteristically raw comments would remain private:

"No one ever goes on about the times John hurt ME. When he called my music 'Muzak.' People keep saying I hurt him, but where's the examples, when did I do it?... Could I have hurt John 'more than anyone in the world'? More than the person who ran [his mother] down in a car?[37]"

Tug of War was Paul's first album after that unlicensed therapy session, and while not directly about John, the title song could easily be a metaphor for the unfinished feelings within the Lennon-McCartney relationship. The lack of specifics in the lyrics makes it a stronger reconciliation plea, in my judgment, than the very on-

---

[36] Norman pleads his case in the introduction to *Paul McCartney: The Life*.

[37] Davies's authorized book on the Beatles, written in 1968, is a fascinating time capsule, half because it was written while the group's members were still obvious chums and half because it contains some of the only interviews with key family members. Just as revealing as his main text, though, are the introductions and postscripts to the book's reprinted editions. A partial transcript of Davies's call with Paul appears in the 1985 version and beyond.

the-nose Lennon tribute "Here Today" from the same set of tunes. Beatle fans can hear it and make it be about John and Paul. But you and I can hear it, close our eyes and have it be about any rocky, confusing, haunting, unresolved and ultimately meaningful relationship of our choice.

My only quibble (and I'm not the first person to say so[38]): Contrary to the language in the background vocals, I'm not sure there's much pushing in a tug of war, only pulling. Right?

"Stranglehold"

(Paul McCartney-Eric Stewart)

Artist: Paul McCartney

Year of Recording: 1985

Appears on: *Press to Play*

Paul admits to not always knowing which songs are his best, so he'll typically play a bunch of new tunes to his kids and their friends to figure out what to release. On occasion, that means a McCartney album won't sound like a McCartney album and will come across instead

---

[38] The author Andy Miller might've been the one. He analyzes the full album on an episode of Chris Shaw's joyous *I Am the Eggpod* podcast.

as a nod to whatever might be playing on modern radio.

The *Press to Play* album from 1986 is generally perceived to be the main example of this pandering, given it's very '80s production. But minus the saxophones, the opening cut, "Stranglehold," jumps out at me, fueled by cool, swaggering guitars and bass and some ferocious drumming.

From my retrospective vantage point, the album's poor reputation is at least partly the result of public complaints from its participants. Guitarist Eric Stewart (of 10cc fame) wrote half of the songs with Paul and assumed—not unlike Elvis Costello after him—that he'd get to produce the record. Instead, Paul latched onto what the kids of the day were into and hired Hugh Padgham (who'd worked with the Police, Phil Collins and XTC, among others) to supervise the sessions. Stewart dissed Padgham's contributions in the press, and Padgham dissed Paul, claiming the material was weak and therefore needed various levels of studio trickery to attract the ear. When told a particular song wasn't up to snuff, Paul took offense and demanded, "Hugh, when did you write YOUR last number one?!?[39]"

---

[39] Padgham was a source for Howard Sounes's *Fab*, one of the better career-spanning McCartney books due to not only what it contains but what it leaves out. Sounes seems to take his

The project bombed, fingers were pointed in multiple directions, and Paul didn't have enough confidence to put out a new set of songs for three years. I'd wager, though, that new fans who hear it without any context/anti-'80s baggage will find a lot to dig.

"Taxman"

(George Harrison)

Artist: The Beatles

Year of Recording: 1966

Appears on: *Revolver*

Paul fell into the role of bass player for the Beatles, but his preferred spot in the band would've been as lead guitarist. Upon joining with John Lennon in their school-era band, the Quarrymen, Paul was given the opportunity to solo on the instrumental "Guitar Boogie" and flubbed it, a rare case of a crowd giving him an attack of nerves instead of confident energy. Paul says the experience kept him from soloing in concert again until well into middle age[40].

---

journalistic role seriously without including flashy details for the mere sake of a good story.

[40] A self-deprecating story told by Paul in the coffee-table book for *The Beatles Anthology*, although it's hard to believe he didn't do any instrumental showboating during one the Beatles' formative, hours-long sets in German nightclubs circa 1960-1961.

Such self-consciousness was apparently far less crippling in the studio. Even with George Harrison bringing in his own song, the solo on "Taxman" is actually Paul. (Same, by the way, for much of the lead guitar during the sessions for *Sgt. Pepper's Lonely Hearts Club Band* , as George temporarily gave up guitar in favor of keyboards and Indian instruments.)

Find me a more blistering and modern-sounding solo than this one prior to its recording in mid-1966, months before anyone had heard of Jimi Hendrix[41]. Go ahead ... I'll wait ...

"My Dark Hour"

(Steve Miller)

Artist: The Steve Miller Band

Year of Recording: 1969

Appears on: *Brave New World*

I'm unaware of any serious observer who'd dispute that the Beatles' breakup was hastened (not necessarily caused) by the death of their fiercely loyal manager, Brian Epstein. When the band recruited for help with business matters toward the end of their run, they picked a tough, blustery New Yorker named Allen

---

[41] "Taxman" was recorded in the spring. Paul would hear Hendrix for the first time in the fall.

Klein, who'd renegotiated record deals lucratively for the Rolling Stones.

So, who was Allen Klein? Well, here's one story: In 1970, George Harrison got hit by a copyright infringement suit because his "My Sweet Lord" sounded like the girl-group hit "He's So Fine." Klein managed George back then and went to the "He's So Fine" people to smooth things out. It didn't work, and Klein was dismissed by George in 1973 for unrelated reasons.

George ultimately lost his copyright case to the tune of $1.6 million. But before the money could change hands, the rights to "He's So Fine" had been purchased by (wait for it) Allen Klein, who bought them after being sacked and might've had a pretty good idea of what the song would be worth[42].

Paul hated Klein and wanted the Beatles to be managed by his future in-laws Lee and John Eastman. Although the conflict of interest seems obvious there, one of the under-explored questions in Beatles history is why they couldn't find a compromise between Paul's family (who ultimately made him the world's richest rock star) and someone he despised (who ultimately went to jail for tax evasion). It's not as if there weren't any other

---

[42] For a deep dive on the "My Sweet Lord" chaos, listen to the "All Things Must Pass at 50, Part 2" episode of the *Nothing Is Real* podcast..

rock managers who'd want to work for the biggest act around[43].

One Friday evening while recording for *Let It Be*, Paul was confronted by Klein and the other Beatles with a management contract. Klein claimed he needed Paul's signature right away in advance of a board meeting the next day. Paul called "bullshit" and refused. Klein was asking for 20 percent of the group's earnings, but Paul insisted that 15 percent was a fairer number for an act of their stature and, besides, why not wait until Monday when his attorneys could be there? John, George and Ringo backed up Klein's demands and accused Paul of stalling.

Feeling cornered, Paul retreated to another studio in the same building, this one occupied by the Steve Miller Band. Looking to blow off steam, he joined them on bass and took out his aggression on drums for "My Dark Hour." Miller would use big pieces of the song a few years later when crafting the hit "Fly Like an Eagle."

Paul never signed and spent the next several years in and out of court, trying to disentangle himself from

---

[43] While Brian Epstein was still alive, the Beatles had vehemently opposed a plan to hand them off to Epstein protégé Robert Stigwood, who'd go on to manage Cream, the Bee Gees and others. Paul also proposed Richard Beeching, former chairman of British Railways, but didn't get anywhere.

Klein and going so far as to sue the other Beatles as a last resort. He'd be proven right by the law and by history, but his friendships with the other three would never recover.

"Young Boy"

(Paul McCartney)

Artist: Paul McCartney

Year of Recording: 1995

Appears on: *Flaming Pie*

At an eighth-grade dance, some friends somehow got it in their heads that I wanted to shake a leg with an admittedly very nice girl from our class. I didn't want to, partly because I'm not the dancing type (then even less so) and because I'm gay (now even more so). After I'd already told them no, they came back and tried harder to pressure me into it. "I said NO. Now, leave me alone!" I didn't realize they'd gone behind my back to arrange something and that this poor young lady had overheard my strong reaction without knowing the context. After I paced one lap around the gymnasium to calm down, I saw her crying in the corner. Being a mature gent, I didn't say anything to her and waited for my mom to pick me up.

That night, a new McCartney documentary premiered on VH-1 in conjunction with Paul's album *Flaming Pie*.

I watched it on repeat long past midnight, feeling equally confused and awful. My favorite from that set remains "Young Boy," and I remember it resonating way back then, even though I didn't have words yet to admit exactly why. "He's just a young boy looking for a way to find love…Nothing you can say will help … it can take so long …"

Paul is an exceptionally positive person, so it's impressive that his advice here is more knowing than a cliché like, "Just put yourself out there." At nearly any age, the heart, hormones, sexuality, etc., are so maddeningly complicated. Or as a certain wise man once said, "Love isn't silly at all."

Stereotyped as pushy and picky within bands, Paul seems willing to give his kids the space to discover themselves. His own "young boy"—son James— followed him into music without leaning on family fame[44] and comes across as awkwardly shy in front of the press, not at all like the father. His daughter Mary mainly took after her mother by devoting herself to photography and vegetarianism. Paul's adopted daughter, Heather, has lived quietly with a talent for pottery.

Only fashion designer Stella, Paul's middle daughter, has shown a willingness to tolerate celebrity. If Paul

---

[44] James plays guitar on "Heaven on a Sunday" from *Flaming Pie* and "Back in the Sunshine Again" from *Driving Rain*.

appears at public events with any of his children, it's likely with her. Upon being inducted into the Rock and Roll Hall of Fame in 1999—not in time for his late wife, Linda, to witness it—he brought Stella onstage and pointed to the message on her shirt: "About Fucking Time!"

"Long Leather Coat"

(Paul McCartney-Linda McCartney)

Artist: Paul McCartney

Year of Recording: 1991 and 1992

Appears on: No US/UK album release (CD single only)

Paul and Linda became vegetarians and animal-rights champions in the 1970s when a sheep approached their kitchen window as they chowed down on leg of lamb. Linda was known to be tough-as-nails on the issue, and you can hear it in 1993's "Long Leather Coat," which blurs the line between activism and assault without apologies. It's a rare legit co-write between the spouses, their first in decades.

The song comes from the sessions for the *Off the Ground* album, an uncharacteristically political work from the eager-to-please Paul. A B-side from the same era chastises political leaders for "fucking it up for everyone," and another track, "Looking For Changes," goes after scientists who experiment on animals ("bastards," as Paul calls them).

A pre-show video for the subsequent tour showed disturbing images of animal testing, including a shot of a cat with a machine wired into its brain. Some paying customers in every crowd likely told Paul to shut up and play the hits, but he defied them by sticking with his wife and including "Looking For Changes" early in his set. "Long Leather Coat," however, (a stronger song on the same topic) got cut from the album except in Germany and the Netherlands and was never showcased to a live audience.

"Say, Say, Say"

(Paul McCartney-Michael Jackson)

Artist: Paul McCartney and Michael Jackson

Year of Recording: 1981, 1982 and 1983

Appears on: *Pipes of Peace, All the Best, Pure McCartney*

"John and I didn't know you could own songs," Paul said to biographer Barry Miles. "We thought they just existed in the air."

As songwriters, Lennon and McCartney basically got half the royalties when one of their tunes was covered by another artist, licensed in a commercial or sampled in a film. The other half, though, plus the right to deny permission for that licensing or sampling, went to music publishers. In other words, to somebody else.

Post-Beatles, Paul would become the richest rock star around, not merely by selling a ton of records but also by buying the publishing rights to other songs. He owns the Buddy Holly catalog, "Chestnuts Roasting on an Open Fire" and all the songs in *Grease*. But until recently, he barely owned any of what he wrote with John Lennon.

Beginning in late 1981, Paul collaborated briefly with Michael Jackson. "Girlfriend," from Michael's *Off the Wall*, was allegedly written specifically for him by Paul, even though Jackson rejected it for four years before doing a version at the suggestion of producer Quincy Jones. "The Girl Is Mine," their duet from Jackson's *Thriller*, is an embarrassingly hokey ballad, steeped in the naivety of barely pubescent romance and with apparently very little input from Paul. But "Say, Say, Say" gives us two legendary singers in prime voice.

During the recording, Michael asked Paul for business advice, and Paul told him the real money was in publishing. "I'm gonna buy YOUR songs," Michael said, and they both laughed. They chatted about it again later, and Michael made the same comment. "I'm gonna buy YOUR songs." Paul assumed it was a joke (and that Michael had forgotten he'd already told it) and chuckled politely, albeit a little less than the first time.

Meanwhile, the rights to the Beatles' catalog went up for sale, and Paul learned he could probably buy them for a little over $30 million. Feeling a bit awkward about the possibility of owning what might—in an alternate universe—have been John's share, he got in touch with Yoko Ono and asked whether she wanted in on it. Paul says Yoko thought the asking price was too high and insisted on negotiating it down to about one-fourth of what had been floated[45]. No deal.

Jackson purchased the songs a few years later as part of a nearly $50 million package. Paul was furious at first, then wondered optimistically if his relationship with Jackson would net him a fair price for what he often calls his "babies." Instead, "Revolution" showed up in a Nike commercial, "All You Need Is Love" was the soundtrack for a Panasonic ad, and "Good Day Sunshine" was used to sell Oreos.

Paul made a big deal publicly about the supposed cheapening of the songs' reputation on account of the ads. "Revolution" was about revolution, he argued, not selling sneakers. Of course, losing out on half the royalties couldn't have felt good either.

A rumor that Jackson had left the songs to Paul in his will proved to be a silly myth. For the most part, Paul

---

[45] Yoko disputes Paul's telling of the story, much of it appearing in Ray Coleman's *McCartney: Yesterday & Today*, written with his cooperation.

has bit his tongue when asked about the experience. But he'll share his memory of the "I'm gonna buy YOUR songs" comment. And when he does, he'll do it in an exaggerated imitation of Jackson's high voice and let out a sly smile.

"This One"

(Paul McCartney)

Artist: Paul McCartney

Year of Recording: 1988

Appears on: *Flowers in the Dirt*

Without much of a story behind its creation, "This One" qualifies regardless as my all-time favorite McCartney song, the ultimate reminder to always consider when it's best to be principled and when it's right to be pragmatic in our most important relationships. It's a cautionary message—easier said than done—about having enough discipline to not become overly emotional in an argument, not lose control of a delicate conversation due to pride, and not box a partnership into a corner where it needs to end unless you're absolutely sure you want out. The lyrics are wise words that are made even wiser by the last verse, which flips the story around, changes the pronouns and makes it clear that the responsibility for maintaining perspective doesn't just belong to the singer but also to his muse.

I keep a reproduction of Paul's handwritten draft in the hallway of my apartment, hoping the sentiment will be fresh enough in my head and heart whenever it might be applicable. Oddly enough, the bridge section actually came first and was slated originally to open the song rather than populate the middle. It's evidence to me that those words were viewed as the emotional core of it all[46] and not just a well-crafted connector from chorus to verse.

Paul played this every night on his '89 comeback tour. And although it bombed as a single, I'm awaiting its rediscovery as Paul at his best: Mature messaging disguised within sunny melodies.

"Band on the Run"

(Paul McCartney-Linda McCartney)

Artist: Wings

Year of Recording: 1973

Appears on: *Band on the Run, Wings Greatest, All the Best, Wingspan (Hits and History), Pure McCartney*

Band on the Run wasn't the first great McCartney album. (That would be *Ram.*) But it took until then for the rock press to stop blaming Paul for allegedly breaking up the

---

[46] I've avoided including the exact section here solely out of copyright concerns.

Beatles and calm down long enough to give his solo music a fairer shot. He'd made four critical flops on his own and knew he needed the kind of big hit that George Harrison had accomplished with *All Things Must Pass* and John Lennon had achieved with *Imagine*. Hoping for inspiration from a change in scenery, he asked his record company for a list of all locations in the world where it owned a recording studio and picked the most far-out option: Lagos, Nigeria.

Two weeks before Paul and Wings were scheduled to fly out, their lead guitarist called it quits due to a combination of musical differences and financial complaints. Then, just a night prior to departure, their drummer phoned and said he was staying home, believing it would be best to postpone the work until they'd brought in a new player and gotten some time to gel. Rather than cancel the trip, Paul boarded a plane and made a vow: "Screw you. I'm gonna make an album that you WISH you were on.[47]"

Early in their stay—and in the middle of monsoon season—Paul and Linda were jumped on their way back to their lodgings, and Paul had a knife put to his throat. In retrospect, those familiar with the situation have acknowledged that Paul only survived because he was white and therefore deemed incapable by locals of

----

[47] Paul in conversation with Dermot O'Leary in ITV's *Paul McCartney & Wings: Band on the Run.*

identifying his black assailants to authorities. Instead, the five men who attacked him stole all the demos intended for the album and presumably trashed or erased them without a clue as to their priceless contents. They've never been recovered in any form.

When the band made it to the Lagos studio, they found a primitive setup without any sound booths. At one point, Paul fainted and was feared to have had a heart attack but likely collapsed from severe stress. Meanwhile, although he'd held out hope that his former bandmates would eventually show, they never did, and he picked up the slack by playing the drums, lead guitar, bass and most of the keyboard parts himself. When the sessions were over, he had a record that sounded way bigger than the three-person credits would suggest. And despite all the turmoil to get it made, it had a cathartic sound to it and a theme of relieved freedom.

When Paul and Linda returned home, they found a letter from their record company. Its message: "Cholera outbreak. Don't go to Lagos under any circumstances."

"Silly Love Songs"

(Paul McCartney-Linda McCartney)

Artist: Wings

Year of Recording: 1976

Appears on: *Wings at the Speed of Sound, Wings Greatest, Wingspan (Hits and History), Pure McCartney*

John Lennon wasn't wired to say nice things about people unless he truly meant them. On Paul's approach to the bass, he offered in one of his last major interviews:

"Paul was one of the most innovative bass players that ever played bass, and half the stuff that's going on now is directly ripped off from his Beatles period ... He's an egomaniac about everything else, but his bass playing he was always a bit coy about. He is a great musician who plays the bass like few other people could play it.[48]"

Given that "Silly Love Songs" is considered to have one of the most impressive basslines in popular music but was written in response to Lennon characterizing McCartney as a lightweight, I wonder what John ultimately thought of it. To me, though, the real highlights are the gleeful horns right after the defiant

---

[48] To David Sheff in *Playboy*.

"Love isn't silly at ALL (yeah, yeah)," the three-part "round" harmony section between Paul, Linda and Denny Laine starting at the 4:30 mark, and then straight back into those horns at 5:12.

In total, it's nearly six minutes that are either free of cynicism or full of fantasy, depending on your mood. But I suppose that if the comparatively less sentimental John can get credit—deservedly—for telling us to imagine a world without greed or hunger, there's little fairness in mocking Paul for a chorus made entirely of "I love you" on repeat.

"I've Just Seen a Face"

(John Lennon-Paul McCartney)

Artist: The Beatles

Year of Recording: 1965

Appears on: *Help!*

For business reasons, until 1967, the Beatles' U.S. albums had completely different track listings than their U.K. counterparts (an inconsistency not corrected until the advent of compact disc reissues in 1987). The soundtracks for *Help!* and *A Hard Day's Night* were half Beatles music and half orchestral film scores in America but full-blown rock albums in England. And in the most egregious example, the version of *Revolver* originally issued in the States only had two of the five Lennon songs from the British release. (Envision that record, the band's best in my opinion, without "I'm Only Sleeping," "Dr. Robert" or "And Your Bird Can Sing." Actually, don't bother. It'll be too painful.)

Despite little interest in how the band wanted their own music presented to the masses, the American record executives somehow stumbled upon an accidental concept album when they messed with 1965's *Rubber Soul*. Instead of kicking the record off with the rocker "Drive My Car," they opened with Paul's acoustic square-dance number "I've Just Seen a Face," which had been buried on the second side of *Help!* in Europe. The move set the tone for what became known as the band's response to folk-rock and got young fans thinking John and Paul had become captivated by L.A. groups like the Byrds and a newly electric Bob Dylan. In reality, it was likely just a matter of an anonymous record-company hack rummaging through a stack of available Beatles material and accidentally creating a mixtape that sounded like a coherent, unified statement.

"I've Just Seen a Face" was perfectly pleasant in the minds of British audiences, but for Americans it became identified with the first "serious" Beatles album, the one Brian Wilson of the Beach Boys played again and again and served as his main motivation for creating the classic *Pet Sounds* set. And of course, it was

Pet Sounds that made Paul want to outdo Wilson by making *Sgt. Pepper's Lonely Hearts Club Band*. Had the U.S. version of *Rubber Soul* contained more electric songs like the British collection—and had "I've Just Seen a Face" not set the mood as track one—it's not crazy to assume *Pet Sounds* would've never happened and, therefore, no *Sgt. Pepper* either. The so-called "Summer of Love" in 1967 might've either had to become synonymous with the Monkees, the Association and the Box Tops or maybe settled on a different nickname.

"For No One"

(John Lennon-Paul McCartney)

Artist: The Beatles

Year of Recording: 1966

Appears on: *Revolver*

Paul dated actress Jane Asher for five years, starting when he was only 20 and she just 17. Near the start of the two's relationship, the Beatles were tired of making several seven-hour trips back and forth from home in Liverpool to work in London. While George, Ringo and John ultimately moved to their own places in the quiet suburbs, Paul wanted to stay in town where '60s culture was about to boom, and the progressive Asher family gave him his own room in their attic.

Jane was a recognized beauty and a serious thespian on stage and screen, but Paul seemed even more enamored with her live-in relatives. Mr. Asher was a world-famous psychologist, and his wife was one of Britain's most esteemed music teachers (even giving oboe lessons to a young George Martin). Meanwhile, Jane's brother Peter was a musical sponge not unlike his sister's boyfriend and had success as half of the duo Peter and Gordon before producing and managing James Taylor and Linda Ronstadt. In a class-conscious England, working-class Paul ate up the intellectual conversations at the family dinner table, attended classical concerts with Jane and treated those early-to-mid-'60s as an extended education and self-improvement project.

Much of what has been discerned about the relationship with Jane from Paul's perspective has been picked out of his love songs from the era, and most of the ones known to be about her frankly make Paul out to be a bit petty, immature and possessive. Future wife Linda would inspire adoring ballad after adoring ballad. Jane, on the other hand, influenced the two-faced "I'm Looking Through You," the pouty "You Won't See Me" and the ultimatum "Another Girl.'

"For No One," not at all a picture of romantic bliss, is still Paul's most mature take on his presumed first try at real love. It's resigned in its sadness and more matter-of-fact than judgmental about the end of a connection, even as it narrates only from the man's point of view. The couple would break up two years later after Jane literally walked in on Paul with another woman as if he nonchalantly wanted to get caught.

Jane has barely said a word about Paul since then, and Beatles historians are divided about whether they want her to change her mind. Of course, they'd love to know her perspective on such a key piece of her and Paul's life. But getting her to talk would break a commendable streak of discretion and independence[49]. Paul has followed her lead and spoken fondly of the Ashers without betraying much privacy.

As for the then-secret girlfriend discovered in Paul's bed, you're damn right *she* wrote a book.

"Spies Like Us"

(Paul McCartney)

Artist: Paul McCartney

Year of Recording: 1985

Appears on: *Press to Play* (1993 reissue only)

Paul isn't a magically great songwriter. He's a gifted worker bee who treats his art like a job. If most of us were to write a song per day, we'd max out with a few

---

[49] Even the supremely respected Mark Lewisohn hasn't snagged a formal sit-down interview.

of them achieving passable status. Paul can follow a similar schedule, starting from his own baseline level of talent, and surprise no one by occasionally hitting upon what sounds like a classic.

Sometimes, though, he'll wrap up a stinker for a famous fan and offer it as a gift, such as the title tune for somebody's movie. Case in point is 1985's "Spies Like Us," a jaw-droppingly sad contribution to a lame Chevy Chase flick that's even sadder when you realize it'll probably be the very last Top-10 hit single of Paul's legendary career (Kanye West team-ups excluded).

Paul says the song was commissioned by director John Landis, who claims he accepted the tailor-made turd on the basis of studio pressure and his own fanboy nerves. "To me, the Beatles were like Christ …" Landis explained in a colorful interview clip[50]. "I just completely folded. And now I'm thinking, 'What the fuck am I gonna do with this song?!'"

Landis compromised by lifting the up-tempo final minute—the sole sign of life—and dropping it at the start of the film's closing credits. Beyond that point, he reasoned, most of the audience would've already walked out.

---

[50] https://vimeo.com/231246735

"Temporary Secretary"

(Paul McCartney)

Artist: Paul McCartney

Year of Recording: 1979

Appears on: *McCartney II*

Paul has released three albums with the simple title *McCartney*, the general assumption being that the pieces of the trilogy are connected by having him on every instrument. But given that he basically did the same on *Band on the Run*, *Memory Almost Full* and *Chaos and Creation in the Backyard* (all very good records under their own names), the one-man-band quality is only part of the differentiation.

Unlike Paul's more commercial efforts, the ones with the *McCartney* tag all originated as at-home musical doodles, not intended for public ears at first and not overseen by the pressure of outside crew or producers. They're Paul giving into his personal instincts as opposed to catering to what might be a hit, and they were all made at moments when he was stuck in a challenging limbo. The first record from 1970 came during the dark depression of the Beatles' breakup. The second, from 1980, followed the end of Wings and his traumatic stay in a Japanese jail for marijuana possession[51]. And the third arrived near the end of COVID-dominated 2020 because, well, what else would Paul do during lockdown other than seclude himself at work and wait for inspiration?

Paul's eponymous albums also have a history of confused reactions from fans upon first listen, only to gain in cult status some 20 or so years later. I haven't spent enough time with the third entry to love it, but if I'm still around in 2040, I'll probably claim it's the one to buy.

"Temporary Secretary" is maybe the ultimate *McCartney* homemade track, concocted because Paul was testing a synthesizer-like tool by repeating the same programmed notes again and again and thought it sounded like a typewriter. I first heard it when I was six or seven and knew it was unbearably obnoxious even then. It certainly wasn't proper Beatles music to my ears at that age and had lyrics that were half ridiculous and half creepy. (Why does he need a secretary so badly, and why would he put her on his knee? And what's this talk about paying her well? Paying her for what, exactly?).

It was played first to me on my father's attic-stored turntable, intended as a distraction while I moped my way through exercises for mild cerebral palsy: Up and

---

[51] Some of *McCartney II* was recorded (but not released) earlier than those events.

down a single flight of stairs, careful to land each step on the heel and not the toes.

I was convinced immediately of its awfulness, yet even the smug critic inside my first-grade self couldn't resist Paul's hyper-robotic voice in the bridge. It was the first time I noticed the influence of a song's rhythm on my own body and how as the music accelerated, so did I. I'd never gotten up and down a flight of stairs so quickly and probably haven't since.

A more modern crowd rediscovered "Temporary Secretary" after various DJs slipped it into their club acts. A dear friend of mine got to see Paul in 2015 and, lo and behold, the man who usually refuses to play anything but a greatest-hits concert threw the kids a bone and did a live version of it for the first time. In that context, what I once considered to be one of the worst songs ever made probably sounded like one of the best.

"Leave It"

(Paul McCartney-Linda McCartney)

Artist: Mike McGear

Year of Recording: 1974

Appears on: *McGear*

The strongest album Paul made in the mid-1970s doesn't have his name on it. "McGear" is the stage name of Paul's brother, Mike, who dabbles most famously to Americans in photography and became well known independently in England as part of a musical/comedy group, the Scaffold. Always at least semi-conscious of not wanting to cash in too blatantly on Paul's stature, Mike found a nice compromise on his most notable solo record by enlisting his sibling as producer/writer/bassist but not milking the connection as part of a big-time publicity blitz. Meanwhile, Paul got a chance to write some idiosyncratic material and show off a rarely seen but privately documented playful sense of humor. On the first line of "Leave It," for example, is it "I dearly love her arty jokes" or "I dearly love her artichokes"? The liner notes for the album are written with a grinning wink and let you decide for yourself.

In extended interviews, Mike has an impressive way of being an open participant while also setting careful boundaries. He's the kind of guy who'll say to a reporter, "Sorry. I need to leave in five minutes," and then spend another hour with the person, telling a tall tale like a jovial regular at a local pub, all the while not betraying anything personal about Paul. I'd imagine people walk away feeling so disarmed by his chummy yet slightly off-topic storytelling that they forget to ask anything as intrusive as, "So, what's your brother up to these days?"

A rare exception where Mike addressed his relationship with Paul directly occurred on *The Mike Douglas Show* in 1969. Panelists were pontificating on the "rumor" that Paul had died and that the music industry had covered it all up. And then there was Mike as a surprise member of the in-studio audience basically telling the media to shove it. He'd taken care not to exploit his family name, so it's no shock that he'd take offense at some well-dressed strangers doing it under the guise of journalism.

"On My Way to Work"

(Paul McCartney)

Artist: Paul McCartney

Year of Recording: 2013

Appears on: *New*

If you commute via a long bus ride every day, it's easy to fall deep into your own head. During the best of times, it's a chance to daydream and feel confident that your priorities are in the right place, that the inconveniences of a job are worth it because of what's being built at home or anywhere besides the office. And when there's nothing hopeful on the horizon, being on public transportation for hours at a time—packed into a crowd while minding your own solitary business—is an easy invitation to feel helplessly anonymous and forgotten. As Paul sings about here, it's an environment that can make you wonder, will I ever be seen? How will I ever not be alone? What's available to me in the interim besides (as Paul suggests) the distraction of pornography or (in the age of iPhones) hours of podcasts to block out the fearful sense of stagnation?

Maybe the good news is that a young Paul wasn't sure if he'd ever be important to anyone either but seems to have done okay for himself. Patience, perhaps, can be helpful in the meantime. Being in a rock band and having a fine-enough face to be labeled "the cute one" probably doesn't hurt either.

"Too Many People"

(Paul McCartney)

Artist: Paul and Linda McCartney

Year of Recording: 1970 and 1971

Appears on: *Ram, Wingspan (Hits and History)*

In its 1971 review of *Ram*, *Rolling Stone* deemed the album "so incredibly inconsequential and so monumentally irrelevant … it is difficult to concentrate on, let alone dislike or even hate[52]." What ridiculous

---

[52] The review was by Jon Landau, an otherwise serious critic who later became a bigger deal as Bruce Springsteen's manager. The nearly exact same passages are quoted in Joe Hagan's Jann Wenner biography, *Sticky Fingers*.

and mean-spirited words for what I'd argue (and I'm not alone) is Paul's most characteristically "Paul" album, the one that gives you a sense of what he contributed to the Beatles but also provides examples of his own personal taste. For fans of the Fabs, there are *Abbey Road*-type fragments strung together and a few grand production numbers that you'd never hear from a solo John, George or Ringo. For future fans of Wings, there are Paul and Linda's harmonies all over the place and a flavor of homemade domesticity in both the softer country-influenced numbers and the messy pre-punk rockers. Whether via the arrangements or Paul's big bag of vocal stylings, the songs hop all around as if intended by their maker to say, "I'm ALL of this music rolled into one. Deal with it, folks."

The album was a critical bomb, which likely had more to do with warring Beatle factions than what was truly in the grooves of the vinyl. A marriage of sorts had concluded bitterly, and all the kids in this case—the media and the fans—treated Paul like the uncool parent who'd ruined their illusion of a happy home. When he protested otherwise, it just provoked more anger and relayed messages that nobody was ready to hear.

Ram was Paul and Linda self-righteously against the world, claiming in the chorus of one composition, "We believe that we can't be wrong." It was Paul hitting back against the bogus claim in the press that he'd been the one who broke up everyone's favorite band[53], and it was a brave yet ultimately foolish case in which he took direct aim at John, who'd always have the last laugh in a battle of words.

Paul basically calls John and Yoko a pair of self-important posers "preaching practices" on the record's first song. "You took your lucky break and broke it in two," he finger-waves at John, reminding him that it wasn't Paul who had asked for an artistic divorce. John would hit back even harder on his *Imagine* collection, drafting George Harrison to help him complete the McCartney takedown "How Do You Sleep." ("The only thing you did was 'Yesterday …'") Look carefully at the bugs on the back of *Ram* and, yes, those are literally two beetles fucking each other.

---

[53] In a press kit for his first solo album, Paul was the first to imply a split publicly. John had already left but had been convinced by management to keep quiet until various business deals had been negotiated to the four's best advantage.

"Every Night" (*Unplugged* Version)

(Paul McCartney)

Artist: Paul McCartney

Year of Recording: 1991

Appears on: *Unplugged (The Official Bootleg)*

Paul was back at being a huge touring attraction by the early 1990s but no longer a factor on the charts. He hadn't had a top-20 album since 1983's *Pipes of Peace*, and even after playing to millions to promote *Flowers in the Dirt*, his new music wasn't bringing in new fans.

Without grand expectations, he performed on the *MTV Unplugged* program, where big names showcased allegedly acoustic versions of their typically electric catalog. Most bands cheated and used instruments that still plugged into amplifiers, whereas Paul and company did it raw by placing microphones carefully in all the right places. And rather than roll out the hits, the set was fairly experimental, with blues covers and even the first song Paul ever wrote, "I Lost My Little Girl" (done in public for the first time for the broadcast).

The intimacy of the evening also led to an unexpected emphasis on songs from his no-frills solo debut, *McCartney*, including rare stabs at "That Would Be Something," "Junk," and, best of all, the tranquil breeze of "Every Night." You can hear the audience cheer after the first line, even though the original was never played on the radio. It's just a beloved gem from deep in the Macca canon. Normally, Paul sings, he'd be out on the town as a way to escape his own head. But for now, he just wants to be home with his favorite person. A classic extrovert's embrace of introversion

Afterwards, Paul was the first *Unplugged* artist to release his performance as a full album. Absent any precedent, expectations for sales were so modest that only a few thousand copies were pressed, and the CD was given the subtitle *The Official Bootleg*. Who, after all, would be interested in an aging '60s figure playing relaxed music in place of his best-known material? The album came and went, and Paul remained a dinosaur with a mullet for a while.

But other acts took notice of the *Unplugged* strategy and leaned into it. Nirvana, Eric Clapton, Tony Bennett, Rod Stewart. They all went on the show, cranked out a tie-in album and didn't goof around with any "bootleg" nonsense. All were platinum sellers in the millions. And in the case of Clapton, Stewart and Bennett, the artists suddenly became hip again, capable of stalling their induction into the aforementioned dinosaur category for at least half a dozen years.

Now pushing 80, will Paul have much touring left in him? And if so, is he too attached to the precision of his stadium shows to ever consider an up-close and by-the-fire run of small theaters where he doesn't need to belt out any beloved anthems and can play whatever tickles his fancy? Indeed, that would be something.

"Eat at Home"

(Paul McCartney-Linda McCartney)

Artist: Paul and Linda McCartney

Year of Recording: 1970 and 1971

Appears on: *Ram*

Despite the nastiness exchanged between John and Paul during the 1971 *Ram/Imagine* era, not everything landed like a punch. The two guitarists employed by Paul on *Ram*—David Spinozza and Hugh McCracken—would both later play on some of John's records and not by coincidence. When the heat lessened between the former bandmates, John was willing to acknowledge that if someone was good enough to meet Paul's standards, the same player was likely good enough for him, too.

And while John took offense at many songs on *Ram*, the one with the most obvious reference to him and Yoko Ono didn't make his relationship with Paul noticeably worse. Paul's suggestion on "Eat at Home" that he and his wife ought to "eat in bed" could've easily been interpreted as a swipe against the peace-themed press conferences that the Lennons had conducted in their honeymoon suite while decked out in their pajamas. But John uncharacteristically wasn't bothered by it and presumably took it as either a lighthearted tribute or just Paul and Linda experiencing what he and Yoko were doing in their own blissful newlywed period: Eating at home and in bed and enjoying a spouse's company in other—ahem—more private ways.

When John married his first wife in 1963, a younger Paul was amazed to learn husbands and wives would ever do something as risqué as make love during the afternoon. Six years later, Paul married Linda, and less than two weeks after that, John married Yoko.

For two friends whose relationship was breaking down, it's interesting that they made the same life-altering choice at almost the exact same time. Was it a signal of intense competition between them or maybe some evidence that they were still boys afraid of adult-level changes unless an old pal was willing to take the same risks? The two couples rarely saw each other socially, and the post-Beatles meetings between John and Paul were infrequent and frosty (if not exactly icy). Yet had they been capable of resolving more of their personal differences, how much bonding might have been possible over both having to sustain a marriage under a rock-and-roll spotlight?

"Mumbo"

(Paul McCartney-Linda McCartney)

Artist: Wings

Year of Recording: 1971

Appears on: *Wild Life*

In an attempt—conscious or otherwise—to save the collective of himself, John, George and Ringo, Paul proposed in 1969 that they get back to their roots as a group, play as a foursome without any studio trickery and do an anonymous gig, maybe billing themselves as "Rikki and the Red Streaks" so the intense pressure of being the BEATLES in all caps wouldn't be so daunting. But a miserable time was allegedly had by all during rehearsals, the music suffered, the members went their separate ways before fruition, and Rikki and the Red Streaks went down in history as just a nifty name.

If you want a clue as to how much Paul was impacted by the breakup, consider that he was the one who formed another band within just a year of their official split. The early days of his rebound group, Wings, tried to make good on Paul's last hopes for the Beatles. Their first album was dashed off quickly with no frills, and its cover didn't even specify who was playing on it. No names, no mention of Paul. Just a distant photo of him, Linda, guitarist Denny Laine of the Moody Blues and session drummer Denny Seiwell for anyone willing to squint.

When they toured to promote their debut, Wings drove around in a bus, showed up unannounced at local English universities and asked if they could take over the student union. It might've all been a big test to show the world that Beatle Paul was just one of the guys, not only in love with being around other musicians but perfectly capable of countering the media narrative of him as domineering by checking his ego at the door. People who take themselves too seriously certainly wouldn't open their new act's first release via a song like "Mumbo," with lyrics that can't ever be classified as silly since no one can understand them in the first place.

It was all so daring and yet so dumb. Rather than fresh and exciting, the inaugural output from Wings comes across as under-rehearsed and very much like an unsteady band still in search of its sound. It's one of only two Beatles-related album I bought as a kid and threw away[54]. Paul, Linda and Denny Laine would eventually get there, though, finding a distinct vocal blend to complement Paul's knack for 1970s Top 40 pop singles. Minus a few later exceptions—I'm looking

---

[54] The other was George Harrison's *Dark Horse*, recorded during an obvious bout of laryngitis.

at you, 1979's "Old Siam Sir"—the words would be intelligible, too.

"Eleanor Rigby"

(John Lennon-Paul McCartney)

Artist: The Beatles

Year of Recording: 1966

Appears on: *Revolver, 1962-1966*

"Eleanor Rigby" is the first Paul song on my first Beatles album, *Revolver*, and it spooked me as early as age four. Here was a rock band using cellos and violins instead of guitars and singing about ignored people dying alone rather than a boy/girl chapter in a puppy-love tale. The emphasis on third-person "regular" protagonists instead of first-person confessions is, on its surface, classic McCartney and a style that separated him from the usually more autobiographical John Lennon. But was this actually a McCartney song?

In one of his major yet uncredited contributions to *Revolver*, George Harrison came up with the "Ahhh, look at all the lonely people" refrain, and Ringo Starr gave Paul the details about the priest "donning his socks in the night." John's best friend, Pete Shotton, was also in the room and suggested all the characters in the lyric come together in the last verse, although when they do, it's a sad, missed connection instead of a happily fated union.

John's work on the song is one of only two cases in which the memories regarding credit were very different between Lennon and McCartney (the other being "In My Life")[55]. On one hand, John was said to have been hurt by Paul's willingness to solicit and accept suggestions from people other than him, which supports Paul's claim that John only added a few words to "Rigby." But in major interviews during the solo years, John was also adamant about having written most of the lyrics beyond maybe the first verse. Perhaps stirring up the tension and the misremembered origins was the Beatles' late-career manager Allen Klein, who didn't get along with Paul, needed Lennon as an ally, and would frequently "remind" John that the song was basically his despite Paul being applauded for it.

One documented piece of input from John that Paul rejected was to keep the original name "Father McCartney" in the final version. Wary of fans thinking the tune was about his father, Paul opened a phone book and found a different Irish name, "McKenzie," as a replacement. As for the woman of the title, she

---

[55] John did a song-by-song recount of who supposedly wrote what as part of a major 1980 interview with *Playboy*. Paul did essentially the same within *Many Years From Now*.

was made up, too, albeit influenced by the band's friendship with actress Eleanor Bron from their *Help!* film. But in a Liverpool-area cemetery near where John and Paul undoubtedly hung out as teenagers, a gravestone for an actual Eleanor Rigby had already existed for decades. Where do the lonely people come from? In this case, probably the subconscious mind.

"On the Wings of a Nightingale"

(Paul McCartney)

Artist: The Everly Brothers

Year of Recording: 1984

Appears on: *EB '84*

Paul, unlike most of the other Beatles, found ways as a kid to save up and see concerts in Liverpool. He stayed outside venue entrances with an autograph book and remembers being peeved when he plopped down a large sum to see Bill Haley and the Comets, only to have most of the night taken up by support acts he'd never heard of.

John and Paul both loved the Everly Brothers. Paul's first public appearance, in fact, was a rendition of their "Bye, Bye Love" at a summer-camp talent show. (No, he didn't win.) Later, when the Beatles recorded the acoustic and harmony-filled song "Two of Us" for *Let It Be*, Paul could be heard on certain takes referring to

John as "Phil," as in Phil Everly. And in 1976, he'd name-check both of the brothers on his 1976 hit "Let 'Em In." He'd rarely have reason to be starstruck by anyone from his own generation or later, but when talking about people he'd listened to as a teenager, he speaks with the enthusiasm and experience of having been a young fan.

"On the Wings of a Nightingale" was gifted to the Everlys as part of an early-'80s comeback attempt and is widely considered the best song Paul ever wrote for someone other than himself. For me, the killer moment is the "Oh, I can feel something happening" chorus, where the melody soars like the bird in the title.

Paul often speaks of his experiences at those 1950s concerts when asked about interactions with his own fans. Don't request a selfie or an autograph, but he'll usually stop for a human moment with a nervous admirer to answer a question or hear a story about what his music has meant to someone. Make it a conversation rather than a transaction, and he'll typically engage.

Those early memories of pop idolatry have also supposedly influenced his concerts. Ticketholders will rarely be subjected to a "get-off-the-stage" opening act and, at the time of this writing, he was still giving crowds a two-and-half-hour show with no intermission. He'll play all the hits, too, because he knows how he would've felt if Bill Haley had somehow escaped Liverpool without doing "Rock Around the Clock." As for whether he's thinking about his teenaged self at all when he sets his top-of-the-market ticket prices, well, next question.

"Big Barn Bed"

(Paul McCartney-Linda McCartney)

Artist: Wings

Year of Recording: 1972

Appears on: *Red Rose Speedway*

As a 10-year-old, I entered a trivia contest at a Chicago-area Beatles convention where the players had to buzz in with the name of the first song on a given album. These were one-on-one matchups, and when neither contestant knew an answer, the rest of us in the crowd could yell it out together. To me, these were simple questions, and I was stunned that none of the adults seemed to be treating these facts like sacred scripture. If these people weren't spending hours looking at Beatle records and memorizing which song was on which album, what exactly were they doing with their lives?

When nobody bit on the opener to Paul's 1973 *Red Rose Speedway* collection, I shouted "Big Barn Bed!!!" in my most whiny of voices. But in a lesson in humility, I was ultimately asked to identify track one on the only album (group or solo) that I didn't own, the Beatles' red *1962-1966* compilation, and got knocked out of the competition. Of course, I immediately started crying from embarrassment, and the very nice people who were sorely lacking in their understanding of mildly obscure McCartney fluff gave me a prize anyway, which only made me more self-conscious and had me crying even harder.

"Big Barn Bed" should've been an easy one because it's, in my opinion, the alive outlier on an otherwise dead bunch of songs. Despite silly lyrics about weeping on a willow, sleeping on a pillow and leaping armadillo, it finds a groove and builds upon itself until it becomes a party at full capacity. You can hear bits and pieces of the tune in its infancy on the outros on *Ram* from two years earlier, and how it survived to kick off *Red Rose Speedway* is a sneaky, minor miracle.

Originally intended as a double disc, *Red Rose* got cut down by orders of the record company with an ear specially attuned to what might get played on light AM radio. Everything else that resembled rock got dumped into the archives, and all the twee easy-listening material survived. It was another critical lashing in Paul's early solo career, and one that made his triumph later that year with *Band on the Run* all the more necessary.

None of this is to say that stereotypically stiff industry executives robbed the world of what would've been a masterwork. Producer Glyn Johns, who'd most recently worked on some of the Who's seminal catalog, said of the *Red Rose* sessions, "If you think because you are playing with Paul McCartney that everything you do is a gem of marvelous music, you're wrong, it isn't. It's shite. And if you want to sit and play shite and get stoned for a few hours that's your prerogative, but don't expect me to record everything you're doing, because frankly it's a waste of tape and it's a waste of my energy[56]."

The initially planned double-album has since been made available for collectors, and although I won't say Johns is wrong about the overall quality, the complete set is at least an intriguing marker that shows Paul and his relatively new band taking some experimental risks with soul, glam, reggae and more. In other words, there's more on it besides "Big Barn Bed" to suggest Paul hadn't just turned into your dad.

---

[56] Quoted in *Fab* by Howard Sounes.

"Hi, Hi, Hi"

(Paul McCartney)

Artist: Wings

Year of Recording: 1972

Appears on: *Wings Greatest, Wingspan (Hits and History)*

He may have been the cute, crowd-pleasing former choirboy among the Beatles, but Paul certainly has a healthy mischievous streak. Consider these words that appear either blatantly on his records or deep enough in the mix to avoid prudish detection:

- The background vocals on "Girl" that go "tit, tit, tit."
- The original line in "Day Tripper" that went, "She's a prick teaser …"
- The detail in "Penny Lane" about indulging in "fish and finger pie."
- Paul's seemingly good, giving and game attitude toward pleasing his female partner in "Eat at Home" and all the talk about "eating in bed."
- His 2018 dirty-grandpa single "Fuh You."
- The first woman in "Maxwell's Silver Hammer," who's studying at home and is "all alone with a test tube, oh, oh, oh, oh."
- And of course, the harmlessly virginal "Why Don't We Do It in the Road?"

By the time of "Hi, Hi, Hi," Paul had already gotten a song banned by the BBC ("Give Ireland Back to the Irish"), and it's amusing to note what he was willing to say openly in its lyrics and what he still felt necessary to obscure. He references a "sweet banana" and even calls the song "Hi, HI, Hi" for crying out loud during the peak of his extended pot habit. He's also ready to "do you," and "like a rabbit" to boot.

But then there's this bizarrely coy section that starts, "I want you to lie on the bed and get you ready for my…POLYGON?!?!." At least, that's what Paul still swears he's singing and certainly not, not, NOT "body gun."

Nonetheless, the folks running British radio didn't buy it, and the perceivably squeaky-clean contributor to the Fab Four got nailed with his second banned single in the same year. So much for writing silly love songs.

Besides the censored "Give Ireland Back to the Irish" and "Hi, Hi, Hi," Paul's only other single from 1972 was a version of "Mary Had a Little Lamb." He says his decision to release a nursery rhyme had absolutely nothing to do with those bans and definitely wasn't a commentary on being shamed as a very naughty boy by the government airwaves.

Uptight puritan that I am, I prefer to believe him and go back to my innocent early Beatles records, like the one with the request to "please please me, like I please you."

"Put It There"

(Paul McCartney)

Artist: Paul McCartney

Year of Recording: 1988

Appears on: *Flowers in the Dirt*

Jim McCartney didn't know how to read music, but he was a good-enough self-taught player and showman to serve as a semiprofessional bandleader around Liverpool. When he had children, he encouraged them to learn an instrument because, in his wisdom, those were the people who always got invited to parties.

Even after giving up on show biz and going back to selling cotton, Jim would tinker at the family piano, purchased at a shop owned by none other than the grandfather of future Beatles manager Brian Epstein. The tune he kept coming back to the most was written on his own and called "Walking in the Park With Eloise." In the 1970s, Paul remembered the melody and had it released under a different name as a surprise to his dad. When Paul reminded Jim of the song, the senior McCartney replied modestly, "Oh, I didn't write that! I just made it up!"

Jim was among the more supportive of Beatle parents. That and his absence from home until the evenings made Paul's house a common hangout for a teenage John and Paul as they tried writing their first songs in the living room, smoking tea leaves through Jim's pipe. When they did one of the world's first takes of "She Loves You" in front of him, he said it was very nice but had too many annoying Americanisms in the lyrics. Instead of "She loves you, yeah, yeah, yeah," he pleaded, couldn't it be "She loves you, yes, yes, yes"?

For reasons understandably too complicated and private for him to ever reveal, Paul didn't attend Jim's funeral. But he did write "Put It There" with his father in mind some 10 years later. It's sweet and simple as a tribute, but I prefer to hear it as a broader message against unhealthy grudges and in favor of reconciliation, maybe between family members, perhaps between friends or former romantic partners. Paul assured us with the Beatles that we could work it out, and here he is on his own—cynics be damned—doubling down on the same message.

"Oh! Darling"

(John Lennon-Paul McCartney)

Artist: The Beatles

Year of Recording: 1969

Appears on: *Abbey Road*

I've seen a lot of Beatles tribute bands in my time, and the best McCartney impersonators (Mitch Weissman from the *Beatlemania* stage show, Eric Michaels of the Chicago-area group American English) tend to make "Oh! Darling" a personal showcase in their set. By doing such a raw-throated belter every night, they're way braver than the man they're portraying.

The vocal heard on *Abbey Road* took at least a week to record, with Paul believing he only had one good take in him per day. He'd show up early before anyone else, do a single try with engineer Alan Parsons, say, "Nope, not good enough" and wait until the next session for another attempt. And though he threw some physically demanding Little Richard covers into many of his solo concerts, he's never gambled by doing "Oh! Darling" on stage. Minus rare outtakes, the howling intensity of the original will be his lone and lasting statement on it. John Lennon—a tough critic—shrugged his shoulders and wanted to sing it himself.

"Dear Prudence"

(John Lennon-Paul McCartney)

Artist: The Beatles

Year of Recording: 1968

Appears on: *The Beatles*

Paul and Ringo once performed together at a benefit for the David Lynch Foundation, which funds the teaching of Transcendental Meditation in schools as a way of calming high-risk children. Whereas the two surviving Beatles are fairly private about their continued endorsement of taking 20 minutes twice a day to breathe in, breathe out and focus on a mantra, the late George Harrison was an outspoken follower of TM and its originator, the Maharishi Mahesh Yogi. Had George lived, I'm almost positive all three of them would've played a few old songs there for charity, even though they'd otherwise dissed decades of reunion requests from bleeding-heart causes.

The Beatles latched onto the Maharishi around the time of Brian Epstein's death. Paul studied TM in India for about six weeks, longer than Ringo and family (who had issues with the food and the flies) but shorter than John and George. John gave up on the Maharishi when a friend told him an unsubstantiated rumor about sexual inappropriateness between the jolly host and some of the female guests, but Paul wasn't fazed by the talk. He'd gone to India to learn something, had accomplished his goal and wasn't expecting an infallible hero. George left around the same time as John but regretted it terribly and seemed bitter about the other three's perceived lack of devotion to the training. It's a likely important clue as to why he soured on the band quicker than the others.

The Beatles wrote some 40 songs while in India, despite George chastising Paul to stop plotting their next album and focus on the nature around them. "Dear Prudence," from John, was among them and might be the most compassionate, sweetest item in their catalog, a selfless plea for a hermit-like friend (Mia Farrow's sister) to trust her gifts and be a participant in life rather than an observer. The rhythm section here— the bass and even the drums—is supposedly all Paul, following a brief walkout by Ringo that was prompted by McCartney being a bit too bossy about how the beat should be played.

An old comment—"Ringo isn't the best drummer in the world. He's not even the best drummer in the Beatles"—was long attributed to John, who, even in his most flippant mood, never would've believed such craziness. It's a misquote from British comedian Jasper Carrott that took on a cruelly unfair life of its own. Still, if it IS Paul thumping away at the end, it's hard not to be impressed.

"Friends to Go"

(Paul McCartney)

Artist: Paul McCartney

Year of Recording: 2005

Appears on: *Chaos and Creation in the Backyard*

Paul brought George Harrison into the Beatles after learning about his obsession with guitars from their rides together on the local school bus. There's a telling moment in the *Anthology* documentary about the dynamics of their relationship and why, perhaps, George didn't express eternal loyalty to his childhood chum.

While talking about George, Paul says, "I think he was about 1 ½ years younger than me. That's quite a big age difference at that time, so I used to talk down to him a little bit, as you do to a kid who's 1 ½ years younger than you. When he's 14 ½ and I'm 16. It might've been a failing of mine."

Even as he acknowledges his errors there in dealing with George, Paul actually furthers them by getting the chronology wrong and making himself look better. Paul was born in June 1942, and George in February 1943, not even close to a year and a half apart. As George was fond of saying well into their 50s, "He was always nine months older than I am. Even now, he's STILL nine months older than I am[57]."

After George passed away, Paul tried to imagine what kind of song his mate would've written and came up with "Friends to Go." It lacks any direct lyrical references to him, but its breezy style would fit well on a Harrison album, and its story about a guy who wants to be alone with his crush rather than be bothered by a crowd is in line with George's obsession with privacy and the likely extrovert/introvert clash between the Beatles' bass player and their lead guitarist.

The Harrison family has been understandably tight-lipped regarding the exact date and location of George's death from lung cancer. Some 20 years later, though, there's an unofficial understanding that a gravely ill George had been in Los Angeles for experimental treatment and had hoped to fly back in time to die in his beloved Hawaii but was too sick to get through the long flight. Instead, the family made last-minute arrangements to keep him in California, where—some reports say—he died in a home leased by Paul.

---

[57] Both quotes in this entry come from *The Beatles Anthology*.

"Beautiful Night"

(Paul McCartney)

Artist: Paul McCartney

Year of Recording: 1996 and 1997

Appears on: *Flaming Pie*

Paul has a talent for intriguing endings to his songs. Consider, for instance, the poetic last line on "The End" from *Abbey Road*, the faked outro to "Let 'Em In," or the guitar-heavy last seconds of my all-time favorite McCartney composition, "This One." But the track that goes out with the biggest bang is 1997's "Beautiful Night."

Paul started the song in the mid-'80s and recorded a first try with Billy Joel's backing band before deciding something was missing. The end product, finalized a decade later, found what was lacking and gives us arguably McCartney at his lyrical worst but otherwise (the structure of the song, the playing on it, the production) at the top of his game. If you can make it through lines about getting "a medal from my local neighborhood," too many insertions of the word "love" in the same phrases, and lazy rhymes of "night" with "night," you'll be rewarded with the dramatic buildup of the bridge section around the 2:10 mark, which seems at first like an unfulfilled tease until the song BURSTS OUT at 3:35.

At that point, there's Paul cooking on lead guitar. There's Beatles producer George Martin arranging the horns. And, oh, who's that not only playing the drums but singing along at the end to "Beautiful night, beautiful night, beautiful night"? Ringo!!!

When the surviving Beatles reconvened for a few songs as part of their *Anthology* project, they insisted on augmenting home demos by John Lennon. It was respectable work performed reverently but unavoidably eerie, ghostly and often lacking in joy. The last segment of "Beautiful Night" suggests what a real Beatles reunion could've/should've sounded like. It's 90 blissful seconds during which all is peacefully right with the world.

"I Saw Her Standing There"

(John Lennon-Paul McCartney)

Artist: The Beatles

Year of Recording: 1963

Appears on: *Please Please Me*

In an effort to convey the Beatles' charisma on record, George Martin wanted their first album to be made live in concert from the cramped, smelly underground Cavern Club, where the group was a staple of Liverpool lunchtime entertainment. Technology being what it was in 1963, the idea didn't get far, but the in-person spontaneity was preserved on purpose by having Paul do an enthusiastic count-in on "I Saw Her Standing There," the first song on their first LP in both the United Kingdom and the United States. The initial American version on *Introducing the Beatles* (a rare release that came out on a small Chicago label instead of the usual Capitol Records) botched the intro by editing out the first few seconds but still kept Paul's rocking yell of "FOUR!"

A decade later, John and Paul were meeting in Los Angeles during the former's 1973-1974 separation from Yoko Ono. According to Paul, he'd met with Yoko and discussed whether she and John would ever get back together. She told Paul her conditions, and he passed them along to John, thereby giving his friend the information he'd need to make a choice about his romantic future and ultimately a decision that changed the short remainder of John's life. According to Lennon's girlfriend May Pang, the former bandmates also made tentative plans to regroup in New Orleans, where Paul was set to make *Venus and Mars* with Wings.

Before the planned meetup with Paul could happen, Lennon made a cameo at an Elton John concert, singing "Lucy in the Sky With Diamonds," "Whatever Gets You Thru the Night" and "I Saw Her Standing There," saying the last number had been written "by an old, estranged fiancée of mine called 'Paul.'" Outside of a brief television appearance the next year, it was the last song John Lennon ever performed for an audience.

Yoko was in the crowd that night and met John backstage. They moved back in together, conceived a child and stopped making music for the next five years. So, after all the supposed animosity in the 1970s between John and Paul/Paul and Yoko, does Paul—of all people—deserve at least a fraction of the credit for saving the Lennons' marriage, or was it all a bunch of coincidences?

Regardless, John's rededication to his home life brought him back permanently to New York City. The plans to connect with Paul in New Orleans were off.

"Distractions"

(Paul McCartney)

Artist: Paul McCartney

Year of Recording: 1988

Appears on: *Flowers in the Dirt*

Paul and Linda played around the world in a rock back together for nearly the first 10 years of their relationship and then spent a decade mainly at home. Many parts of *Flowers in the Dirt*—the album that eventually brought them back out on the road—read like the thoughts of a mature man who's had a lot of space to consider his marriage in honest terms. The arguments on songs like "Rough Ride" and "Figure of Eight" are tough and stubborn and sound exhausting without necessarily indicating that the feuding sides have given up on each other. "We Got Married" ends with the lived-in advice from Paul near his 20th wedding anniversary that matrimony won't run on its own and requires attentive maintenance.

"Distractions," from the same collection, confirms that for this couple, the effort of commitment remained worth doing. It acknowledges a distance that has settled via the passage of time and the inevitable intrusion of everyday minutiae, but it remembers what's special about these neglectful lovers without framing their bond in the past tense. The specialness is still there and ready to be nurtured all over again. If only…

Minus Paul's 1980 stint in jail, Paul and Linda weren't apart for more than a few stray evenings during their 29 years as spouses, and their union was often cited as an impressive model that countered the stereotype of short-lived celebrity romance. Not that they ever claimed it was easy.

As Paul told biographer and friend Barry Miles in the 1990s, "We were very up and down … You get this picture of us swanning along in a little rowboat managing to avoid the white water, but we were right in the middle of that white water, man, so it's even more miraculous that we made it. But we did[58]."

"Uncle Albert/Admiral Halsey"

(Paul McCartney-Linda McCartney)

Artist: Paul and Linda McCartney

Year of Recording: 1970 and 1971

Appears on: *Ram, Wings Greatest, All the Best* (US version only), *Wingspan (Hits and History), Pure McCartney*

For ultimate proof of the once-reviled *Ram* album's revisionist rise to the top of cherished McCartney albums among vinyl-loving twenty-somethings, consider the use of its lead single in Noah Baumbach's film *Greenberg*. We know Paul and particularly his "Uncle Albert/Admiral Halsey" are cool again because a character played by Greta Gerwig—an actress with enough can't-put-your-finger-on-it charisma to star in a remake of *Annie Hall* someday—can be seen rocking out to them alone in her modest apartment.

The song wasn't a new discovery and actually was Paul's first number-one hit as a solo artist in the United States. But how the heck did record buyers in 1971 ever go for such a schizophrenic oddity with the attention

---

[58] From *Many Years From Now*.

span of a nine-year-old? On one hand, it introduces itself as a funeral-like apology from a young generation to an all-but-forgotten elderly man. But then Paul dons a series of goofy hats, does one upper-class-twit accent after another and piles on a set of side effects in the style of "Yellow Submarine," most of which come from his own mouth. Linda's harmonies line up with the initial tone of sadness, but then poor Albert is pushed abruptly out of sight/out of mind, and we're onto the next shiny object, the sunny singalong of "Hands across the water/Heads across the sky!" Imagine an audience waving its arms along to that bit. In fact, imagining is the best you can do because the eager-to-please Paul has somehow never done this big seller in concert. Ever.

Weird as it is, maybe it caught on in 1971 because it was actually Paul's most Beatles-esque offering since their demise. The suites on *Abbey Road* were only two years old at that point, and here was McCartney following up with more fragments that wouldn't have mattered on their own yet somehow project a certain charm as a combined hodgepodge.

"Here Today" (*Amoeba* Version)

(Paul McCartney)

Artist: Paul McCartney

Year of Recording: 2007

Appears on: *Amoeba Gig*

The day he learned of John Lennon's murder, the workaholic Paul coped by heading into a recording studio as scheduled and tinkering with an obscure B-side called "Rainclouds." Unable to focus, the musicians left early, and a dazed Paul was cornered by the press while getting into his car. Asked for his reaction to the news, he stumbled by saying, "It's a drag," and drove away. It was another case (like "What will we do without her money?" when told of his mother's death) in which he'd knock himself for perceived insensitivity when the real culprit was almost certainly nerves in the face of trauma. Alone at home, Paul processed his pain and the guilt over such an understatement by composing a poem about Lennon's killer and named it "Jerk of All Jerks."

The status of John and Paul's friendship by that time was ambiguous. The bright side of history tells us stories about the two of them socializing occasionally in the mid-1970s when McCartney came into New York with Wings. Those tales are countered a bit, though, by their last in-person conversation, during which an annoyed Lennon chastised his former bandmate for wanting to pop in on short notice and told him they weren't kids anymore who could just hang out with no planning. At the "Rainclouds" session, Paul confided to Denny Laine, "I'll never fall out with anyone again for that amount of time[59]."

Even a much older Paul has admitted he sometimes questioned the genuineness of their relationship and whether the affection he still felt for John had long been a one-way street. He'd need to look at warm, old photographs of the two of them to talk himself out of his doubts and conclude, "Yes, we really were friends."

Paul's tribute to John, "Here Today," was a hit when it emerged in 1982 and has become an immovable part of his concert setlist since 2002. Its predictable presence in the show (along with his ukulele cover of "Something" for George Harrison) has seriously diluted its impact by now, but there are still versions on which you can hear Paul becoming choked up. The best of those appears on *Amoeba Gig*, a surprise performance at a famous California record store with the same kind of human intimacy and magic as the bar scene of his viral appearance on James Corden's "Carpool Karaoke" segment from CBS's *The Late Late*

---

[59] Sounes has a short version of this quote from Laine. Doyle includes a longer one.

Show. "We're grownups," he assures the audience after the last note. "We can cry if we want to."

"1882"

(Paul McCartney-Linda McCartney)

Artist: Wings

Year of Recording: 1972

Appears on: *Red Rose Speedway (Archive Edition* only*)*

I'm not sure if "1882" is any good, but beyond the homemade experiments on the *McCartney* trilogy, it's maybe Paul's most bizarre song. Telling of a servant boy who steals to feed his mother, it's played by Wings in a menacing, eerie tempo as if they're setting up a ghost story. And although the character could be a blond-haired Dickensian type forced into indentured servitude, I like to imagine a *Twilight Zone* scenario in which a modern white male falls asleep and wakes up as a terrified black child just after the Civil War and can't find a way back. Sort of *12 Years a Slave* with time travel.

A previous entry in this book mentions the *Red Rose Speedway* sessions and how a double-disc got knocked down to a single record to please squares who preferred AM radio. Unsurprisingly, this one didn't fit into the final strategy and was relegated to obscure bootleg status until surfacing as a bonus track on a 2018 special reissue.

"Daytime Nighttime Suffering"

(Paul McCartney)

Artist: Wings

Year of Recording: 1979

Appears on: *Wingspan: Hits and History*

During a rare case of writer's block, Paul needed to fill the B-side of a single and told each of the other members of Wings to go home for the weekend and come back Monday with their own ideas. May the best song win. Given the financial rewards involved with being named on even the flip of a McCartney 45 in the late 1970s, everyone gave it a shot, even Linda. Of course, the boss included himself in the competition, too, and took his own victory lap by turning in "Daytime Nighttime Suffering."

Paul would later refer to it on multiple occasions as one of his personal favorites, and I'm glad it exists. But what are we to make of his proposal to his so-called bandmates and the fact that he opted to essentially punch them all out in an unfair fight? Was it condescending confirmation that Wings was always just a backup group for Paul and never, in his own mind, a true collective unit worth a damn? Or, as suggested by some fans/amateur psychologists, maybe the whole point of the contest had been for Paul to motivate himself again and contrive the kind of "I can do better than you" rivalry that had proven so productive for him and John Lennon.

Either way, the A-side (see the next entry) made it into the Top 5 in the U.S. and U.K. charts, and the writer of the B-side (Paul) netted royalties based on sales of 500,000 copies.

"Goodnight Tonight"

(Paul McCartney)

Artist: Wings

Year of Recording: 1978 and 1979

Appears on: *All the Best, Wingspan (Hits and History), Pure McCartney*

It's equally surprising that it took the chart-conscious Paul until 1979 to dabble in blatantly disco-influenced dance music and that, heard today, "Goodnight Tonight" stands up as a groovy record rather than an ultra-dated embarrassment. Other rock stars of his era (Elton John, even Ringo Starr) caved into the craze and gave us full albums of the stuff (*Victim of Love* for EJ, *Ringo the 4th* for RS) that weren't even guilty-pleasure charming in their awfulness, and few would've been shocked if a performer as attuned to commercial tastes as McCartney had done the same. Yet this was his main shot at it, and the reaction didn't kill a career or even stall it. In fact, the song's absence from his next album (*Back to the Egg*) likely disappointed buyers and deserved some of the responsibility for that record's underwhelming sales.

I suppose some of the hardcore rock fans who would've otherwise dissed Paul for doing disco had already jumped ship years earlier on account of low-volume ballads like "My Love," "With a Little Luck," etc., and therefore couldn't bash the song because it wasn't even on their radar. But for those who heard it, perhaps what protected Paul from a mutiny by fans was his supremacy with the bass guitar. Disco or otherwise, dance music generally can't succeed without bass, and who would know how to emphasize it better than the world's most melodic player of that instrument?

"Who Cares"

(Paul McCartney)

Artist: Paul McCartney

Year of Recording: 2016, 2017 and 2018

Appears on: *Egypt Station*

I'm not a big fan of 2018's *Egypt Station*, in part because major sections of it sound less like McCartney music and more like Paul acting as a stand-in for his hitmaker producers (Ryan Tedder and Greg Kurstin). "Who Cares" is an exception since it fits Paul's natural status at this point as a rocking grandpa. You can hear the nearly 80-year-old Paul rolling it out as wisdom to a bullied grandchild ("Who cares what the idiots say?") and then wrapping his advice up in the warmest of hugs ("Who cares about you? I do!").

And since grandpas tend to seem cooler to kids than dads, the song's simple message of self-esteem is probably more easily received from this greying, senior version of Paul than via any of his younger selves. From your father, the sentiments might seem corny and cliché. From a father's father, they come across as intended: Pure love.

"Getting Closer"

(Paul McCartney)

Artist: Wings

Year of Recording: 1978 and 1979

Appears on: *Back to the Egg*

After what some deemed a slow start, the Wings of the late 1970s had conquered the world on tour, and Paul had finally climbed high enough on the ladder to qualify as the most commercially successful of the former Beatles. But as the '80s loomed, music had changed. Paul's kids were listening to punk, millions in sales showed that not everyone thought disco sucked, and new-wave acts like Elvis Costello, Talking Heads and Blondie were combining melody with rough edges.

Always one to keep his ear to the ground, Paul retooled his million-selling group with a new drummer and a fresh lead guitarist and seemed intent on making an album with harder rock and a younger sound. The lineup's only album before disbanding, *Back to the Egg*, benefits from crisp production but lacks sufficient confidence to build any momentum. Louder tracks are paired with soft pop, jazz ballads, a hint of country twang and quirky spoken-word or instrumental experiments. Between all that and the dance hit "Goodnight Tonight" (from the same sessions but left off the album), the musicians show they could've played nearly anything and were ready to follow Paul wherever he wanted to go, if only he'd played the role of leader more steadily and picked a direction.

"Getting Closer," though, starts the last flight of Wings already at a high point: The resonant opening chord of the guitars. Paul calling his lover "my salamander" and somehow having such a slithery metaphor come across as a cute compliment.

It certainly ain't punk, but it's muscular power-pop with just enough sugar on top to rival the best work of Squeeze. For a comparison, pit this one against the Difford-Tilbrook collaboration "Pulling Mussels From a Shell" and remember that Paul's version came first[60].

---

[60] Coincidentally, I've bumped briefly into both Laurence Juber (lead guitarist on "Getting Closer") and Chris Difford from Squeeze. They're each very kind when confronted with socially awkward fans having panic attacks in their presence.

"Let Me Roll It"

(Paul McCartney-Linda McCartney)

Artist: Wings

Year of Recording: 1973

Appears on: *Band on the Run, Wingspan (Hits and History), Pure McCartney*

John Lennon, one of the greatest rock singers of all time, loved being the leader of a band but actually hated the recorded sound of his own voice. As the Beatles became more knowledgeable about studio techniques, he'd drive producer George Martin crazy by constantly asking for extra effects to be layered on top of his vocals. Most famously, he ordered Martin to make him sound like the Dalai Lama preaching from atop a mountain on the psychedelic *Revolver* track "Tomorrow Never Knows." More generally, his requests to have his singing bathed in echo were so common that it essentially became a default setting.

When Paul put out "Let Me Roll It" (as in, let me roll you a joint), the consensus was that it was a message to John. The lyrics can be read as a nearly literal passing of the peace pipe between warring friends, and the guitar riff would've fit perfectly on John's rough-edged *Plastic Ono Band* record somewhere between his "Well, Well, Well" and "I Found Out." But what really sparked talk of a Lennon connection was the echo on Paul's voice.

If there's a link between the song and John, Paul says it's subconscious and perhaps a Lennon-esque style that rubbed off on him during their long partnership. Regardless, he clearly adores the tune and has used it consistently as an early number in his live sets. He'll take off his bass for the first time in the show, strap on an electric guitar and, these days, segue from its ending into a look-at-me-go solo from Hendrix's "Foxy Lady."

As for John, he must've thought he was the main influence here. His "Beef Jerky" from a year later ripped off the guitar motif with a jester's smile and the most unsubtle of winks.

"Jet"

(Paul McCartney-Linda McCartney)

Artist: Wings

Year of Recording: 1973

Appears on: *Band on the Run, Wings Greatest, All the Best, Wingspan (Hits and History), Pure McCartney*

There are better songs in the Macca canon than "Jet." Hell, it's about a horny Labrador puppy or a pony depending on which story Paul feels like telling that day. But without it, *Band on the Run* might've had the same fate as *Ram* from a few years earlier, destined for rediscovery by a much younger audience but largely dismissed upon initial release. The album performed with relatively unremarkable results for a few months after its debut, and then "Jet" came out as a single and turned the whole project into Wings' first legitimate smash hit.

Radio finally had a Paul song that sounded huge rather than precious, and nearly all sides of rock fandom could get behind its bipartisan production. The horns, the guitars, the shouts and the simple yet effectively cool synthesizers are the stuff of arena rockers who wouldn't be pushed around. In between, Denny Laine and Linda are "woo-woo"-ing their way through the backing vocals and catering perfectly to a kinder, less intimidating crowd who missed the fun of Beatle music. It usually gets the second slot in Paul's setlist, the same place it appeared on the original album.

"Can't Buy Me Love"

(John Lennon-Paul McCartney)

Artist: The Beatles

Year of Recording: 1964

Appears on: *A Hard Day's Night, 1962-1966, 1*

Paul tries hard to be charming, too hard, it seems, to ever be a good actor. When the Beatles made their first film, *A Hard Day's Night*, each member had a solo scene away from the others to cement his public persona. Those moments helped forever tag George as a bit grumpy, John as a witty rascal and Ringo as the lovable runt of the litter. Something never clicked in Paul's segment, though, and it was stricken from the film with no known archival footage available. In a cinematic context, at least, he'd need to live with merely being the cute one.

The movie's soundtrack, too, doesn't have as much of a Paul presence as expected. The 13-song U.K. version was the first Beatles album to include all Lennon-McCartney originals, but 10 of the baker's dozen were from John. Paul brought in "Things We Said Today," "And I Love Her" and "Can't Buy Me Love."

The latter went through some radical revisions before being finished. It was George Martin who suggested that it start at full force with the chorus instead of a verse or any other intro. And the early takes have awkward call-and-response backing vocals from George Harrison and John instead of just Paul going solo.

The finished recording, despite Paul's general absence from much of the film's storyline, is what plays during the movie's most iconic clip, when the Beatles bust out of a television studio—free from handlers and fans— and run around in a field like a bunch of sugar-high kids at recess.

The two minutes of frolicking have no connection to the plot yet served as important PR for people who weren't sure what this pop group with long hair was all about: At least in 1964, the Beatles were a new brand of youthful energy, they were zany, they were pals and they were having a ball. Watch and listen to us, they offered, and join the party.

"Junior's Farm"

(Paul McCartney-Linda McCartney)

Artist: Wings

Year of Recording: 1974

Appears on: *Wings Greatest, All the Best* (US version), *Wingspan (Hits and History)*

For all the dopey lines about talking to Eskimos and chipping in for bags of cement, "Junior's Farm" won't be denied on account of two seemingly improvised moments from Paul at the microphone: His "giddy-up" scat-singing before the first verse and especially his command prior to the guitar solo, "Take me down, Jimmy!" Imagine being in a band with Paul, getting name-checked on a record and receiving an order from a Beatle to take his song into overdrive.

The "Jimmy" in this case was Jimmy McCulloch, the flashiest lead guitarist in Wings' history. By the age of just 16, he'd already scored a number-one record in

England as part of Thunderclap Newman with the single "Something in the Air," and he seemed to know he was hot enough shit to break lots of rules and temporarily survive the consequences.

During his three years with Paul, Jimmy got into an argument with the boss by refusing to go back onstage for an encore. Around the same time, he caused a postponement in their world tour by breaking a bone during a fight with teen idol David Cassidy. Later, he made Linda cry by breaking into the McCartney family farm and smashing all of her chickens' eggs. Short in stature but with a big mouth, he even picked fights with drummer Geoff Britton, who happened to double as a kickboxing champion. Paul looked past all the unprofessionalism longer than usual because this kid was so good[61].

Wings released two of Jimmy's own songs during his tenure ("Medicine Jar" and "Wino Junko"), both about the dangers of drug addiction. I'm not sure whether those were sung by Jimmy as self-aware warnings to himself or as eye-rolling cases of an addict in denial. Two years after leaving Wings, at age 26, he was found dead at his apartment from an overdose of alcohol and morphine.

---

[61] That is, except for the not-going-back-onstage standoff. Paul pushed back—literally and figuratively—and won that one.

"The Long and Winding Road" (Non-Spector Version)

(John Lennon-Paul McCartney)

Artist: The Beatles

Year of Recording: 196 9

Appears on: *Let It Be: Naked*

Infamous record producer Phil Spector was brought in by John Lennon and George Harrison to clean up what would be released as the Beatles' final album, *Let It Be*, and everyone in the band minus Paul would work with him in some form or another into the early 1970s[62]. The relationship with John would last until 1973, when a paranoid Spector insisted on carelessly wielding a loaded pistol in the control room while hired musicians practiced Chuck Berry oldies.

Paul hated the finished version of *Let It Be* and could've made an easy case that Spector (perhaps with others' encouragement) intentionally sabotaged the best McCartney material on it. To the touching acoustic song "Two of Us" (written for Linda), Spector added an intro in which John jokes about a hungry horse. Before the first notes of "Let It Be" (about Paul

---

[62] George and John used Spector on their own albums. Ringo appeared on those as a sideman.

dreaming of his dead mother), Spector inserted another Lennon spoken-word gag, "And now we'd like to do 'Hark the Angels Come,'" in an exaggeratedly high-pitched squeal.

Paul's biggest complaints against Spector, though, were the heavy orchestra and choir on "The Long and Winding Road." Like it or not, what was intended as a piano-based session of sorrow in the style of Ray Charles was released as a dramatic showtune. Upon hearing it, Paul typed up a letter to management demanding that no one ever mess with his final product without asking and warned, "Don't ever do it again." Paul cc'd his lawyer on the note, and when he later sued the other Beatles to dissolve their partnership, he specifically cited it as an example of him not being allowed to control his own work and getting a damaged reputation as a result. Oddly though, Paul's solo versions of the song (in concert and otherwise) don't deviate much from Spector's pathos-heavy arrangement.

Paul's original vision came out in 2003 as part of the stripped-down remix album *Let It Be ... Naked*. It's the only version I can hear without losing the contents of my stomach.

"Getting Better"

(John Lennon-Paul McCartney)

Artist: The Beatles

Year of Recording: 1967

Appears on: *Sgt. Pepper's Lonely Hearts Club Band*

When Ringo Starr became ill on the verge of a tour, a session drummer named Jimmy Nicol was given the job of temporary Beatle. Asked by the regular band members how he was adjusting to the gig, Nicol would reply reflexively, "It's getting better!"

Paul commonly cites the song "Getting Better" as an easy contrast between his own optimistic disposition and John Lennon's cynical demeanor. "It's getting better all the time," Paul sang to John. "It can't get no worse," went John's comeback. Paul has told the story often enough to warrant eyerolls from fans who've heard at least a few of his interviews. According to Beatles historian and former McCartney employee Mark Lewisohn, people who know Paul well would joke with one another by listening in on a media session and saying something to the effect of, "Oh, he's telling Anecdote #57B in this one[63]." It's a tired tale, perhaps, but one that shatters the myth that the

---

[63] Extensive interviews with Lewisohn can be heard on the "Fabcast" and "Nothing Is Real" podcasts.

Lennon-McCartney writing partnership didn't last into the group's mature later years.

Less discussed is the bridge section about having beaten a woman, being ashamed of it and trying to change. It's a remarkable admission (inserted by John) from a foursome of perceived lovable mop-tops, let alone as part of a pop song in the still very innocent time of 1967. Here are guys in their mid-twenties from traditional post-WW2 backgrounds in a tough British port city owning up to some caveman tendencies and inching their way closer to more progressive values. It's jarring but also maybe a baby step toward John's eventual support of feminism and the peace movement and/or Paul's commitment to animal rights and his waving of the Pride flag at the end of his concerts. It's grownups taking responsibility for their treatment of others and committing to at least a gradual evolution.

"Something"

(George Harrison)

Artist: The Beatles

Year of Recording: 1969

Appears on: *Abbey Road, 1967-1970, 1*

"I think if you have a relationship with somebody else, you have to be able to trust each other. And to be able to do that, you have to be able to talk straight. The thing with Paul is, one minute he says one thing, and he's really charming, and then the next minute he's all uptight[64]." -George Harrison

Post-Beatles, George also once said he'd be in a band with John Lennon any day but never again with Paul. The reasons must've been personal, not musical, because based solely on the recorded output, Paul was the one giving the most to George's songs: the piano and howling backing vocals to "While My Guitar Gently Weeps," allegedly writing the up-tempo bridge to "I Me Mine," and contributing both the essential bass and harmonies to "Something."

John didn't even play on several of George's songs: "Here Comes the Sun," "Piggies," "Long, Long, Long," "Savoy Truffle," "Love You To," and "I Me Mine." Instead, he openly mocked the latter by waltzing around the studio with Yoko Ono, and he generally complained about George's tunes being too hard to play due to their abundance of chords.

Adding to this odd triangle, the only otherwise group performance that Paul never played on was "She Said, She Said," supposedly because John had enlisted George's help to write it and not him. It's from the same album (*Revolver*) that featured the most George

---

[64] Quoted by Chris Mercer (reportedly from a February 1988 interview) on the "Tug of War" episode of the *Take It Away* podcast.

songs up to that point, including the primely featured opener "Taxman." And yet almost immediately afterward, George began withdrawing from the band, nearly gave up playing guitar for a year and only contributed one composition each to the *Sgt. Pepper* and *Magical Mystery Tour* releases.

I'm not the first to wonder if George's increasing lack of interest was sparked by the "She Said, She Said" experience. John took his suggestions but didn't share any of the writing credit or royalties, and Paul had stormed off in a huff. George was finally getting close to his two buddies in craft, and although Paul would get over it and provide support in ways that John continued to withhold, neither of them instinctively cheered him on. "Lennon and McCartney," he must've thought as he began stockpiling his own material for a solo career. "Who needs 'em?"

"So Bad" (*Broad Street* Version)

(Paul McCartney)

Artist: Paul McCartney

Year of Recording: 1983

Appears on: *Give My Regards to Broad Street*

The McCartney family of 1983 was largely female, with Linda plus Paul's three daughters. Paul would say the phrase "Girl, I love you so bad" in half-joking but still sincere fashion to them around the house. But he realized that his kindergarten-aged son, James, felt left out. He reworked the song to include both genders, started saying "Boy, I love you so bad" to James and made the shy kid blush.

Paul released two official versions of "So Bad." This rarer one has an all-star lineup of Paul on bass, Ringo on drums, Dave Edmunds ("I Hear You Knocking," "Girls Talk") on guitar and Eric Stewart of 10cc ("I'm Not in Love," "Things We Do For Love") on guitar and harmonies.

"My Love"

(Paul McCartney-Linda McCartney)

Artist: Wings

Year of Recording: 1972

Appears on: *Red Rose Speedway, Wings Greatest, All the Best, Wingspan (Hits and History), Pure McCartney*

As articulated so well by podcaster Sam Whiles, the problem with "My Love" isn't that it's a silly love song. It's that it's a DORKY love song. The cupboards being bare, still finding something there, woah, woah, woah, woah and all that. Keep your eyes off the lyric sheet, though, and it can be saved (maybe even treasured) thanks to Paul's vocal dexterity and the guitar solo from Henry McCullough.

The good and bad thing about being in a band with Paul is he can handle anything and sometimes believes (maybe rightly albeit rudely so) that he can play your instrument better than you. He'd especially dictate parts to McCullough, who'd either want to go in a different direction or claim that what Paul insisted on hearing couldn't be done. "Oh, yeah?" Paul would think. "Watch me and pay attention."

"My Love" was recorded live with a 40-piece orchestra, and Paul had a solo ready as usual for Henry, who brushed it away and insisted on improvising with the tape rolling and the meter running on the expensive session. Henry pulled it off, and his intuitive take became what every successive McCartney guitarist was forced to emulate whenever the song was played in concert for the next 40 years. But he'd continue clashing with Paul over similar issues and be out of the group within six months. Rather than recruit an immediate replacement, Paul just played the solos on his next album himself.

"Rock Show"

(Paul McCartney-Linda McCartney)

Artist: Wings

Year of Recording: 1975

Appears on: *Venus and Mars*

After a few minor tours of Europe, including one in which they just drove around to colleges in a van and asked to play unannounced, Paul and Wings were confident enough in 1975/1976 for a legit world tour, starting in small theaters at home and ending in huge American stadiums. "Rock Show" helped open each concert and seems to have been written specifically for that purpose. Following years of being dismissed as soft, the band dared to reference decibel meters, Jimmy Page, the Hollywood Bowl, Madison Square Garden and other symbols of larger-than-life, golden-god-like fame. Beatles historian Ken Womack has suggested that those pieces of the lyrics were challenges that Paul and company made to themselves: We WILL be as loud and grand as Jimmy Page. We WILL pack those iconic venues. We WILL be the biggest band in the world and grab the audience by the neck until they forget whatever Paul did in the 1960s[65].

---

[65] Discussed on the "Venus and Mars" episode of the *Paul or Nothing* podcast.

Stick with the original version of the song, and run fast from a blasphemous three-minute edit intended for radio and found on some compilations. You'll miss so many layers of this rich dessert. There'll be no ding-dong bell section after the first minute, no Jimmy McCulloch yelling "Rock show!" and "Long hair!" back at Paul just past the four-minute mark and—oh, what a crime—no outro, starting with the late, great rhythm-and-blues legend Allen Toussaint on piano and highlighted by a strutting spoken-word monologue from Paul. He encounters his mate, reminds the person of an upcoming in-demand concert and brags about having tickets. Then, the possible gender-bending command to put on a dress and a wig, and finally, Paul going, "uh, huh, huh" and having a mini-orgasm at the microphone. If Wings' detractors want to accuse the band of making "granny music," this is the wrong place to start.

"Twenty Flight Rock"

(Eddie Cochran-Ned Fairchild)

Artist: Paul McCartney

Year of Recording: 1987

Appears on: *CHOBA B CCCP (The Russian Album)*

Revered Beatles historian Mark Lewisohn points out that the classic order of "John, Paul, George and Ringo" wasn't a market-tested tagline but an accurate chronological tracking of the band being formed: John brought in Paul. Paul brought in George. And George brought in Ringo.

Paul had seen John in Liverpool neighborhoods and on buses but met him the first time during a break between sets by John's first group, the Quarrymen, at a church festival. Along with Paul being able to tune John's guitar for him, Eddie Cochran's "Twenty Flight Rock" sealed the deal for McCartney and earned him an invitation to join. Paul likely got addicted to the song via the early rock movie *The Girl Can't Help It*[6], and he impressed this undeniably cool older boy by being able to both play the tune and remember all the words.

It says something about John's character that he adored being head of a gang, the unquestioned leader, yet still deemed it important enough to bring on a younger kid who (at least in 1957) had so much more musical polish than him. Instead of viewing Paul as a threat to his dominance, he saw someone who could push their shared dreams forward.

Not that these teenagers were above any power plays. Rather than recruit Paul himself, John relied on a mutual friend to track Paul down on his bike and make

[6] As far as early rock movies go, *The Girl Can't Help It* ranks among the best, largely because it's in bright, energetic color.

the offer. Paul, who must've been dying internally to accept, tactfully waited a few days before saying yes.

Paul played the song again in 1987 as part of a jam session that ultimately helped him pick his late '80s drummer, Chris Whitten. Whereas many pros who audition for Paul expect to do a bunch of Beatles and Wings material as part of their test, McCartney has a habit of keeping the process loose and letting the players find a groove through a series of relatively simple oldies. In this particular case, the entire nostalgic set made it onto a Russian-only collection the following year as a gesture of good will from Paul to a changing Soviet Union. The album title, *Choba B CCCP,* indeed translates loosely as *Back in the USSR* and soon became a hot item among bootleggers. Westerners got an official release in 1991.

"Talk More Talk"

(Paul McCartney)

Artist: Paul McCartney

Year of Recording: 1985

Appears on: *Press to Play*

Some 35 years on, *Press to Play* is still treated like the black sheep among McCartney albums. Producer Hugh Padgham has mentioned a lack of confidence on his part, a clumsy hesitancy to stand up to Paul and a supposedly misplaced trust in studio tricks to mask deficiencies in the material. Fans at the time seemed to agree, viewing it all as too self-consciously "'80s" and making it the lowest-charting standard set in Paul's U.S. career.

Hearing it today, I'd argue (along with writer/podcaster Kit O'Toole) that there's a lot to admire here as Paul dares to take big risks with his sound. It bombed, in large part I'm sure, because it's his least Paul-like album. Erase his familiar voice, and your ears might mistake it for a Peter Gabriel record instead. But given the sorry lack of regular content from Gabriel during all this time, my response would be, "And that's a BAD thing?!?" If Paul and Peter ever want to do anything substantial together, sign me up.

"Talk More Talk" is basically all Paul on the instruments but with some spoken intros from Linda and even nine-year-old James McCartney. According to Paul, the comment "I don't much like 'sitting-down music'" was lifted from an interview with Tom Waits.

"The End"

(John Lennon-Paul McCartney)

Artist: The Beatles

Year of Recording: 1969

Appears on: *Abbey Road*

According to George Martin, the two sides of *Abbey Road* (the last album made by the Beatles, albeit not the last to hit stores) were a compromise, with John's preference for stand-alone songs on one half and Paul's fascination with medleys/mini-suites on the other. Initially, John's favored side was supposed to close the record rather than open it, in which case it all would've ended with "I Want You (She's So Heavy)," a song that doesn't really stop and just runs out of room on the original vinyl. It would've been a deliciously devious farewell from the band, maybe even enough to anger some fans and make them feel cheated for the lack of closure.

Logical heads prevailed, and the proper end to the Beatles output was represented by, well, "The End," which Paul still uses as a goodbye at his nearly three-hour shows. It's a glorious jam from a group that rarely reveled in look-at-us solos. After giving Ringo the spotlight, all three guys in the front strap on a guitar at roughly 54 seconds in and take turns bowing to us with lick after lick. The order is Paul, George, John, Paul,

George, John, etc., and you can hear each player's style. Paul's is melodic, George's is more pensive, and John's is rough and dirty, less focused on technical prowess and more on provoking a feeling.

And then there's the epitaph from Paul, one that sums up all the good feelings communicated via nearly all Beatles music. "And in the end, the love you take is equal to the love you make." From someone who's often mocked for lazy or inconsequential lyrics, it's not merely a career highlight. It's maybe the best parting line in all of rock.

"Good Times Coming/Feel the Sun"

(Paul McCartney)

Artist: Paul McCartney

Year of Recording: 1985

Appears on: *Press to Play*

Post-*Abbey Road*, Paul continued combining bits of songs into one, turning it into a semi-signature move. A partial list of combo material/suites/medleys from his solo career:

• "Hot As Sun/Glasses/Suicide" (1970)

• "Momma Miss America" (1970)

• "Uncle Albert/Admiral Halsey" (1971)

- "Back Seat of My Car" (1971)

- "Long-Haired Lady" (1971)

- "Little Lamb Dragonfly" (1973)

- "Hold Me Tight/Lazy Dynamite/Hands of Love/Power Cut" (1973)

- "Band on the Run" (1973)

- "Picasso's Last Words" (1973)

- "Venus and Mars/Rock Show" (1975)

- "Treat Her Gently/Lonely Old People" (1975)

- "Backwards Traveler/Cuff Link" (1978)

- "Morse Moose and the Grey Goose" (1978)

- "Cage" (1979)

- "After the Ball/Million Miles" (1979)

- "Winter Rose/Love Awake" (1979)

- "The Pound Is Sinking" (1982)

- "Tug of Peace" (1983)

- "P.S. Love Me Do" (1990)

- "Vintage Clothes/That Was Me/Feet in the Clouds/House of Wax/End of the End" (2007)

My favorite McCartney mashup might be "Good Times Coming/Feel the Sun." Both parts began as stand-alone, longer pieces, but they fit together as musical representations of either different summers or maybe even the same season on diverging timelines. "Good Times Coming" is all look-back nostalgia and heat. "Feel the Sun" is immediate, in the present and, despite the fiery star in its name, as cool and refreshing as a pool party. That is, until a young couple sneaks away and one person demands in horny, PG-rated code, "If you love me, show me now!" It's not the most consensual of moments, perhaps, but still destined to be a fond memory for both lovers as part of the "golden summer" referenced in the first half.

It's sadly another track on *Press to Play* that gets bashed for its production and presumably for not sounding much like Paul McCartney. Folks, give me this quartet—with Paul on bass, famed Bowie alum Carlos Alomar on guitar, Crowded House's Eddie Rayner on keyboards and Jerry Marotta of Peter Gabriel's band on drums—and I'm inclined to keep my mouth shut and curved in a smile.

"Yesterday"

(John Lennon-Paul McCartney)

Artist: The Beatles

Year of Recording: 1965

Appears on: *Help!, 1962-1966, 1*

After Paul dreamed the melody to "Yesterday" sometime in 1963, he assumed it was an old bit from decades earlier, maybe something his father had exposed him to as a kid. He badgered everyone he could think of for nearly the next two years, tinkering with it at any nearby piano and asking people where it had come from. He'd test the patience of guests at parties until they'd exclaim, "It's YOURS!" During one such check to see if he'd engaged in subconscious plagiarism, the mother of singer Alma Cogan asked if he wanted some scrambled eggs, and the tune got its first words. "Yesterday, all my troubles seemed so far away" was originally "Scrambled eggs, oh my baby, how I love your legs."

Finally building up enough confidence to claim the song for himself, the otherwise hardly shy Paul realized uneasily that there wasn't much his other bandmates could add, and so he was talked into recording it without the other Beatles, marking the first time they didn't all appear on the same track. It could've been marketed as a McCartney solo single, but Paul wasn't ready for the attention, particularly if it would mean being associated with a creative endeavor so distant from his rock-and-roll reputation. And besides, manager Brian Epstein was generally opposed to promoting one Beatle above the others. In England, to play it safe, "Yesterday" was earmarked as an album track on the second side of their *Help!* LP and not a single for radio. The opposite happened in America, where the band had less control over their releases, and it became a number-one hit.

Paul was initially supposed to play it all alone on acoustic guitar and needed George Martin to twist his arm into allowing classical musicians on the track. A full orchestra would be too tacky, he worried, so they compromised by including a string quartet instead. Paul, who would never learn to read music, was still only 22 at the time and relied on Martin to translate his ideas to the older and more traditionally seasoned session players. He knew what his music should feel and sound like but didn't want to say the wrong thing and come across as the naïve, clueless kid in front of the perceived professionals.

The making of "Yesterday" is a classic case of an undeniably proud Paul—then and now one of the most famous men in the world—nevertheless exhibiting remarkable insecurity. It's a pattern that would continue into key sections of his solo career, when he'd know he was good enough to work with some of the best collaborators available (Elvis Costello, Nigel Godrich, etc.) but was too thin-skinned to withstand their constructive criticism for more than a one-off project. Penning what is often cited as the most covered song in popular music doesn't seem to have relaxed him. If anything, at nearly 80 and still making records, it's sometimes as if he's still trying to prove to himself and others that what he dreamed was more than a fluke. It's an understandable brand of abandonment-tinged neurosis, I suppose, if your lover, your mother or whatever muse you're singing about has to go but doesn't say why.

"Sing the Changes"

(Paul McCartney)

Artist: The Fireman

Year of Recording: 2007 and 2008

Appears on: *Electric Arguments, Pure McCartney*

Paul came up with the concept of *Sgt. Pepper's Lonely Hearts Club Band* as sort of an acting exercise for the Beatles, who were reinventing themselves by quitting the road, digging deeper into studio capabilities and growing mustaches to match. While John Lennon was at the microphone for the sessions, Paul would coach him to not sing like the famous John Lennon but to perform his parts like a doppelganger in the wackily named fictional group.

Beyond the title tune, the lead-in to "With a Little My Help From My Friends," and the reprise that nearly concludes the record, *Pepper* doesn't stick to the Beatles-in-disguise concept and ends up being a meticulously produced set of otherwise unconnected songs. A more realized version of Paul's original plan can be heard in his occasional "Fireman" project, where he and the producer Youth build a song a day largely free from the conventions of pop.

At first, the Fireman name was used to put out nearly anonymous ambient techno pieces sampled from a few of Paul's pre-existing works. The duo's first two collections were hits with critics, and the third was their first to feature prominent vocals and even a mention of who the heck was actually making this music in the first place. Criticized by some in his later career as too much of an oldies machine, maybe Paul had had enough of the putdowns and wanted to make it clear that he was responsible for a perceivably relevant act.

Paul plays everything in the Fireman and sounds liberated while wearing a different costume, like a shy thespian who releases long-repressed emotions via the perfect role onstage. Yet even as he allows himself to make something without the weighted expectations/consumer biases of an official "Paul McCartney" release, his classic gifts can't be obscured. As himself or from behind a mask, the dude knows his way around a melody.

"Figure of Eight" (Live Version)

(Paul McCartney)

Artist: Paul McCartney

Year of Recording: 1989

Appears on: *Tripping the Live Fantastic*

During Paul's first two tours with Wings, he played zero Beatles songs. Then in 1976 and 1979, roughly 1/5 of the setlist dipped into the 1960s. After another 10 years of being off the road, he used his 1989/1990 concerts to embrace his first band's greatest hits, doing half Beatles and half not. Fast forward to his 21st century appearances, and the percentage of Beatles stuff had ballooned to about 2/3 of the show.

Paul will give his casual fans what they want to hear for their high-priced tickets, but I miss his 89/90 attitude, which amounted to rewarding the crowd with the sweetness of an oldie but only after they'd eaten a vegetable or two in the form of whatever music he'd been nurturing in the much more recent past. Although they might've made a face while sampling an occasional Brussel sprout, the concerts' customers were bound to find a carrot or two that they unexpectedly liked.

"Figure of Eight" was a brand-new song in those days, and Paul showed tremendous confidence by having it open each of the 100-plus gigs. Keep in mind, these were huge corporate-sponsored events, often with anywhere from 50,000 to 100,000 baby boomers in attendance. Casual fans would go nuts for "I Saw Her Standing There," "Sgt. Pepper's Lonely Hearts Club Band," "Can't Buy Me Love," "Get Back" and any other familiar rocker they could sing along to, but they'd need to listen for a while before being allowed to lean back into their memories for the rest of the evening.

What they heard first was an introduction to Paul's tight backing band with Robbie McIntosh of the Pretenders on lead guitar, the Average White Band's Hamish Stuart on bass/guitar/vocals and Julian Cope's Chris Whitten on drums. Paul would dance to his right so that the crowd would notice Robbie just before the latter's first solo of the night around the 3:05 mark. Then he'd gallop to his left so eyes would be on Hamish by the time they'd both scream into the same shared microphone. A minute later, he'd put all of them in the spotlight with an order to sing to him as he took a breath.

"Figure of Eight" is now older than Paul's Beatles songs were on that tour, and he hasn't played it since. Somehow, despite all the deserved exposure and a well-mixed version made specifically for radio, it died at #92 on the Billboard Hot 100 singles chart. Will Paul ever feel the itch to scratch his '80s material in a manner similar to his '60s output? I doubt it, but I'd have a happy heart attack upon its return. Me and maybe two other guys in the 100,000-seat stadium.

"My Old Friend"

(Carl Perkins)

Artist: Carl Perkins

Year of Recording: 1981 and 1996

Appears on: *Go Cat Go!*

Even more than Elvis—who did the most well-known version of "Blue Suede Shoes"—the Beatles were perhaps the biggest and most famous supporters of rockabilly star Carl Perkins. They covered his "Honey Don't," "Everybody's Trying to Be My Baby" (a showcase for George Harrison at several concerts), and "Matchbox" on their official albums and then did obscure Perkins numbers like "Glad All Over[67]" on radio appearances for the BBC.

Paul invited Perkins to record with him on the Caribbean island of Montserrat in early 1981, and Carl wrote a song the night before his intended departure as a thank-you for the hospitality. When the McCartneys heard it the next morning, Paul began crying and had to leave the room. Linda told a

---

[67] No, not by the Dave Clark Five.

confused Carl that the lyrics about old friends undoubtedly resonated with Paul, who'd lost John Lennon to murder only two months earlier. Paul and Carl made the basic track later in the day, but it stayed on the shelf for 15 years until Perkins put it out on his final album.

"Calico Skies"

(Paul McCartney)

Artist: Paul McCartney

Year of Recording: 1992

Appears on: *Flaming Pie*

Of being knighted, Paul initially said, "The nice thing about it, really, when me and Linda are sitting on holiday, watching the sunset. I turn to her and say, 'Hey, you're a Lady.' It's nice because you get to make your girlfriend a Lady – although she always was anyway."

Linda died at age 56, a bit more than two years after a diagnosis of breast cancer. Although it was conceived earlier, "Calico Skies" made it onto Paul's final album of her lifetime and was the last of his many great love songs to his first wife.

Unlike so much of his material after the 1970s, "Calico Skies" is commonly unveiled in concert and has even been used as a wedding tune among fans who've kept paying attention. It's not anything that was ever marketed to radio, just a track in the middle of a late-career record that otherwise came and went. And yet it found its way organically into a revered spot in his overall canon. Rightly so.

"I will hold you for as long as you like," he sang to Linda, and he did. After climbing into bed for their last hours together, his final words to her were, "You're up on your beautiful Appaloosa stallion. It's a fine spring day. We're riding through the woods. The bluebells are all out, and the sky is clear blue[68]."

"Veronica"

(Declan MacManus-Paul McCartney)

Artist: Elvis Costello

Year of Recording: 1988

Appears on: *Spike*

The late-1980s pairing of Paul with Elvis Costello might seem, in retrospect, like an effort by the McCartney people to get their man a hit record after a lengthy drought. What's sometimes forgotten, though, is that Costello wasn't a huge seller in America even back then and had only made the Top 40 singles chart

---

[68] Both quotes about Linda in this section come from *Many Years From Now*.

once ("Everyday I Write the Book"). In reality, the return on investment for Paul was more about street cred, whereas the boost in commercial success went to Elvis.

"Veronica," co-written with Paul with a guest spot from him on bass, was Costello's only U.S. Top 20 song and exudes a level of pep that both suits and contradicts its lyrical content. It's about Elvis's grandmother, who we assume was battling lonely dementia-like issues, and stars a woman who now lives in her own head.

If there's comfort in the words, it's from the reminders that she was once young, in love and very much alive. We're told there was a sailor who carried her picture with him on his travels, and dammit if she still remembers his name even though everything else in her brain is presumably one big fog. She's silent in her chair these days, not responsive when her sitters shout her name or steal her clothes, but, Elvis assures us, she was carefree before her mind began to weaken and delightfully mischievous.

Paul and Elvis collaborated on another song, "That Day Is Done," about the same woman but inspired by her funeral. When Paul suggested the arrangement should sound like the synth-pop band the Human League ("Don't You Want Me"), her famous grandson had to leave the building and count to ten to avoid blowing his top. Paul relented, but the story, detailed in Elvis's memoir, is maybe a peak into the McCartney/Costello dynamic. They clearly like and respect each other. (Elvis played at Linda's public memorial and was a special guest at the White House when Barack Obama gave Paul the Library of Congress Gershwin Prize.) But they were both already very famous upon meeting, confident in their instincts and maybe too stubborn to succeed in most bands without being top dog.

"Another Day"

(Paul McCartney-Linda McCartney)

Artist: Paul and Linda McCartney

Year of Recording: 1970 and 1971

Appears on: *Wings Greatest, All the Best, Wingspan (Hits and History), Pure McCartney*

Upon being the first member to announce the Beatles' breakup (albeit not the first to actually quit), Paul didn't help himself among the pissed-off public by releasing "Another Day" as his debut solo single. George Harrison was doing grand arrangements with Phil Spector. John Lennon was putting out raw and personal rock like "Cold Turkey" and "Working Class Hero." And here was Paul, providing a breezily arranged but narratively downbeat song about a lonely and anonymous office worker.

It was attacked for being too light at the time, but take it as a metropolis-set version of "Eleanor Rigby[69]," an admirably empathetic salute to someone who can't be noticed long enough to qualify as a participant in life[70]. In the morning, we have a character who can't stay awake, and by the evening she can barely find an incentive to stay alive. Some 25 or so years later, the band Fountains of Wayne would tell this sort of woman to try a reset in their tune "Sick Day," but she's not just coping with something that bed rest and an afternoon of relaxed binge-watching will straighten out. This is her normal, and it won't change without some luck.

Beatle geeks like me have an annoying habit of assuming all of John's lyrics are about Paul and all of Paul's lyrics are about John, as if neither man ever had another important relationship after going their separate ways in their late twenties. This one, though, gets namechecked in John's 1971 putdown of Paul, "How Do You Sleep." ("Since you've gone, you're just 'Another Day.'") John's dig was further evidence of the rock world being underwhelmed by Paul's effort in the

---

[69] Drummer Denny Seiwell has made the same connection between the two songs.
[70] For a male-centric version of "Eleanor Rigby," sample the gorgeously sad "Footprints" from *Press to Play*. Its co-writer Eric Stewart made the comparison first.

context of the time. Critics were as dismissive of him as they were of the nearly suicidal people in his songs.

While listening today to John's "(Just Like) Starting Over" (the last hit of his lifetime), I bumped on a section that author/podcaster Robert Rodriguez has also underlined on various occasions. In three consecutive lines, John talks about spreading "wings," not letting "another day go by" and assuring his audience, "my love, it'll be just like starting over." Wings? As in Paul's band Wings? Another day as in THIS other day? My love, as in the gooey number-one single "My Love" by Paul McCartney and Wings? Starting over, perhaps, with Paul?

Well, let's just say those are too many coincidences in a row for me, particularly given the chronology. "Starting Over" is from 1980, recorded just months after John heard Paul's "Coming Up." For more about how it all could connect, if only we lived in a land of fan fiction, flip back to the first song featured in this text.

146

"No More Lonely Nights (Ballad)"

(Paul McCartney)

Artist: Paul McCartney

Year of Recording: 1984

Appears on: *Give My Regards to Broad Street, All the Best, Wingspan (Hits and History), Pure McCartney*

During the brief period between John Lennon's death and the rise of Michael Jackson's *Thriller*, Paul was arguably the world's biggest pop star. He must've felt invincible, and 20th Century Fox must've believed it too when they agreed to finance his own film, *Give My Regards to Broad Street*, to the tune of nearly $10 million.

What might've worked as an hour-long music video goes on for another 45 minutes or so and makes the critical error of trying to tell a thin story. Something about lost tapes of a new McCartney record and how greedy corporations will take over if the songs aren't found ASAP. It's not a turkey exactly, but only because it's too dull to reach a level of humorous embarrassment. Paul of the Beatles, one of the most charismatic acts of our time, spends a lot of time driving alone in his car or walking the streets in longshots. You can't complain about what happens because nothing ever does.

"No More Lonely Nights" shows up late to add drama to one of those walking-around scenes, and it might be the last of "classic" Paul. At 42, he was still capable of singing the hell out of it. And while the tune itself satisfies the emotional requirements for an '80s power ballad, the arrangement doesn't trip into showtune schmaltz. David Gilmour of Pink Floyd fame performs two scorching guitar solos, the best of which is allowed to dominate from 3:50 onward and gives the song muscle to match its heart.

The movie grossed only $1.4 million at the box office and set Paul up for a crisis of confidence for nearly the rest of the decade. Roger Ebert called it a "non-movie" in his one-star review. When Ebert's TV colleague Gene Siskel saw Paul in person, Paul asked him what he thought of the film. Siskel said it was "horrible, everything about it" and nearly had a glass of orange juice thrown in his face.

"Off the Ground"

(Paul McCartney)

Artist: Paul McCartney

Year of Recording: 1991 and 1992

Appears on: *Off the Ground*

After his successful comeback tour of 1989/1990, Paul took most of his backing musicians into the studio and made his first "band" album since the breakup of Wings. The production on the *Off the Ground* collection is generally clean and unfussy, the stuff of a tight gang knowing what they're doing and not messing around or overthinking the job. There's a sense that most of the material was arranged with the intent of it being recreated easily by the same players at the next round of large venues.

The title song is at least a semi-exception in that its basic rhythm parts were contrived on computers before Paul added a human presence. All the uncool "la, la, la"-ing in the chorus made it a private, shameful pleasure for me as a teenager. But the more I mellow out in adulthood, the more I appreciate and even lean on it for comfort. The guitar gets a cathartic workout, we get some happy chords, and Paul cuts though all the BS that distracts or paralyzes us by focusing simply on the only logic or math that should matter. He and the listener, Paul reasons, both "need loving." So, don't worry about appearances or embarrassing yourself, and let's do this.

"Ballroom Dancing" (*Broad Street* Version)

(Paul McCartney)

Artist: Paul McCartney

Year of Recording: 1984?

Appears on: *Give My Regards to Broad Street*

Young Paul was both a popular kid and a teacher's pet. He'd kiss up to his instructors by asking them about their lives, and his classmates would be fine with it because it was all a plot to control the clock and avoid being assigned any work. His talent for charm and knowing when to summon it no doubt helped him as a young and hormone-driven man, too. The famous Paul McCartney was polite and quite capable of winning over any girlfriend's mother, but the real Paul wasn't sexually naïve or as squeaky clean as advertised.

Paul's ability to play to both sides can be heard on the re-recording of "Ballroom Dancing" (done first for *Tug of War* and again for the aforementioned *Broad Street* soundtrack). The 1984 version starts as pleasant and G-rated entertainment, shifts toward an edgier punk sound after getting the parents on Paul's side and then goes back to the dancehall arrangement once the kids are onboard. Everyone hears what they need to hear from one of rock's most skilled politicians.

"Mistress and Maid"

(Paul McCartney-Declan MacManus)

Artist: Paul McCartney

Year of Recording: 1991 and 1992

Appears on: *Off the Ground*

Paul's songs with Elvis Costello succeed in large part because they feel complete in their storytelling. It's not just that Costello can be verbose. (Anyone can whip out a thesaurus and go nuts.) It's that the verses, bridges and choruses build upon one another rather than merely continuing a basic theme in search of more rhymes.

When we meet the heroine of "Mistress and Maid," she's essentially all alone, sharing space with a partner who barely looks at her anymore. But instead of wallowing in pity, the lyrics put her in action. She pleads for attention and intimacy. And when using her words doesn't change the situation, she stays in motion, and her needs lead to consequences. There's a beginning, a middle and an end.

Paul sat on this particular collaboration for five years after making a sparse acoustic demo with Elvis. What came out is much more theatrical, with a 15-piece orchestra and an-off balance waltz that dilutes but doesn't entirely disguise the cold tragedy being told.

The McCartney people eventually dug into the archives and pulled out the original recording for high-paying collectors, but the quality from a scratchy cassette isn't so hot. If the song will live on—and I hope it does, perhaps via another singer who discovers it here—the over-produced official version will need to suffice.

"The Fool on the Hill"

(John Lennon-Paul McCartney)

Artist: The Beatles

Year of Recording: 1967

Appears on: *Magical Mystery Tour, 1967-1970*

Paul liked the social and academic aspects of school just fine but bristled at being told what to do. As an adult, he didn't care to be managed either.

Paul was the last Beatle to arrive at the band's first meeting with Brian Epstein, who was ready to offer his services to the locally popular but otherwise stagnant group. While the other three hung around the neighborhood near Brian's office with plenty of time before their scheduled discussion with their future manager, Paul chose to head across town to his home first and made the easily rattled Epstein furious on account of the tardiness. Brian insisted that George call Paul and learn what was taking so long. Told their power-conscious bass player was taking a bath, the testy businessman complained that Paul was very late. There was a comedic pause before George broke the ice with "Late but very clean."

You'd assume the rough, iconoclastic John Lennon would've given Epstein the most trouble during the latter's stewardship of the band's career. Yet in his otherwise whitewashed autobiography, Brian admitted it was Paul who put him under the most pressure and was the hardest member to please. When Brian died of an accidental overdose in 1967, the workaholic Paul acted resiliently and was likely the most convinced of the Beatles' ability to oversee their own affairs. For better or worse, it would be Paul from then on who would call the others up and dictate when it was time to make another album. More than anyone in their last few years as a unit, he worked the hardest at keeping the Beatles together, even as his leadership style (bossiness to some) contributed to their eventual separation.

The *Magical Mystery Tour* film was the band's first major creative endeavor after Brian's passing and Paul's figurative first chance to drive the bus himself. Now that we know not to expect a narrative, are okay with music videos and have been exposed to bizarre Monty Python-esque skits that aren't at all intended to make sense, the movie plays just fine. Viewers who saw it for the first time in 1967, though, and expected a fun-loving romp in the style of *A Hard Day's Night* reacted mostly with bafflement and sleepiness. Worse yet, the color production went out to its BBC home audience in monotonous black and white. It was the first public sign that the godly Beatles were mortal men.

Ringo supervised the cinematography and had the biggest acting role in the picture, whereas John and George largely divorced themselves from the non-musical aspects of the production. Paul took responsibility for the editing, the basic storyline and most of the directorial duties. By extension, he also absorbed most of the blame.

Without *Magical Mystery Tour,* though, we would've missed out on clips of John's "I Am the Walrus" and Paul's showcase "The Fool on the Hill." In that sense, some of the best trades are the ones you don't make.

"World Without Love"

(John Lennon-Paul McCartney)

Artist: Peter and Gordon

Year of Recording: 1964

Appears on: *World Without Love*

When Brian Epstein telegrammed the Beatles to share news of their recording contract, he requested that they "rehearse new material." John and Paul had dabbled in songwriting since their teens. When advertising themselves to booking agents in early 1960, they'd claimed to have written more than 50 tunes. Of course, the same documents overstate Paul's age as 18 (really 17) and say he was attending Liverpool University as an English literature student. It was either PR or BS depending on your favored letters, and so, too, was the size of their self-penned repertoire at that point. Over the next two years, they sprinkled three or four of their own numbers into their extended setlists but were mildly embarrassed by them and usually only brought them out in front of friendly home crowds. Otherwise, by the time of the telegram, they were the best cover band in England but a cover band nonetheless[71].

Somehow, though, Epstein's ask for "new material" was taken to mean "original material," and so Lennon-McCartney got busy and very good, very quickly. Paul especially seemed to be playing the long game. Rock bands weren't supposed to last, and as early as 1963—before he'd even made it to America—he was telling interviewers that his and John's plan was to transition away from performing and into crafting music for other singers. Pretty soon, every act who became friendly with the band was thrown a leftover that John or Paul (mostly Paul) had dashed off and deemed not up to snuff. "It's for You," "Love of the Loved," "Tip of My Tongue," "One and One is Two." If you haven't

---

[71] All a summary from *Tune In* by Mark Lewisohn.

heard any of those, consider your time already well spent.

"World Without Love" was one of the supposed 50 songs from 1960 but never made it into the band's rotation for reasons including the first line. Upon hearing the melodramatic "Please lock me away ..." from Paul, John would lose control in a fit of mocking laughter. The recipient ended up being Peter Asher, the brother of Paul's then-girlfriend and one-half of the duo Peter and Gordon. It was the only non-Beatles Lennon-McCartney composition to top the main U.S. singles chart in the 1960s. If Peter thought the lyrics were accidentally funny, he and Gordon laughed all the way to the bank.

Oddly enough, the first person (Beatle or otherwise) who scored a chart entry with a Lennon-McCartney song in America was Del Shannon with "From Me to You" in 1963, and the best Peter and Gordon hit wasn't "World Without Love"—sorry, folks—but "I Go to Pieces," written by Shannon.

"All My Loving"

(John Lennon-Paul McCartney)

Artist: The Beatles

Year of Recording: 1963

Appears on: *With the Beatles, 1962-1966,*

These days, Paul likes to say the Beatles refused to come to America until they'd scored a number-one record there. And although they would achieve it coincidentally by the time of their first appearance in New York on *The Ed Sullivan Show*, the trip and the gig had been booked months in advance. The fee of $10,000 total for three consecutive episodes wasn't much, but Brian Epstein got them top billing on a hugely popular variety program that reached beyond a teenybopper audience. The publicity was priceless.

An estimated 74 million people and nearly 60 percent of all U.S. television sets saw the band's U.S. debut, and their first look was disproportionately Paul-centric. The inaugural song played, and therefore the inaugural Beatles song likely heard by most people beyond a certain age, was Paul's "All My Loving," and it's amazing in retrospect that the group's record company in the United States never capitalized on the memory of the moment by releasing it as a single. It's one of the few times for Paul when the lyrics were conceived first and the music second, which might explain the easy flow and rhythm to the words. Only the "you" and "true" rhyme comes across as lazy today, and it's a nitpicking criticism when you consider the song's overall tightness, including George's country-western solo and John's motoring rhythm guitar.

Next, they played "Till There Was You," a showtune for the parents and again with Paul on lead vocals. And then as an unfair reward for driving the opening number along so well, John got to sing "She Loves You" at a microphone that barely picked up his voice. They took a break and finished with Paul's "I Saw Her Standing There" and "I Wanna Hold Your Hand," another intended John showcase that emphasized too much Paul due to the aforementioned equipment problems. John's biggest moment of the night came when the production team inserted a caption under his image: "Sorry, girls. He's married."

"Hope of Deliverance"

(Paul McCartney)

Artist: Paul McCartney

Year of Recording: 1991 and 1992

Appears on: *Off the Ground*

If you somehow grew up watching as many afterschool reruns of the super-safe sitcom *Full House* as I did, you might recall the time when Uncle Jesse got a record deal and became a big star … only in Japan.

Weird musical successes that somehow do or don't translate across the oceans are a real thing. In Paul's case, he'd had a brief revival in 1990 as a bigger-than-God touring attraction. A few short years later, though, he was back to being an out-of-style Boomer act. "Hope of Deliverance" was the lead promotional single from *Off the Ground*, and it stiffed at #83 on the weekly Billboard Hot 100 chart in America. Yet the song rocketed into the Top 10 in Austria, Canada, Belgium, the Netherlands, Italy, Denmark, Germany, Iceland, Japan, Norway, Switzerland and Poland.

Did it resonate—as supreme Macca podcaster Chris Mercer has hypothesized—due to the post-Cold War changes in so much of Europe in the early '90s? Or was it as simple as those audiences being less uptight than me and my fellow Americans and more willing to embrace an unabashedly sunny message? Paul and his band will likely never play this in L.A., Chicago or New York. But scream it out during a soundcheck in Hungary or Brazil, and they just might oblige.

"Got to Get You Into My Life"

(John Lennon-Paul McCartney)

Artist: The Beatles

Year of Recording: 1966

Appears on: *Revolver*

Paul was the last of the Beatles to dabble in hard drugs. The others had tried LSD months before and had been pressuring him to join in, but he'd heard stories about people's lives being altered forever by their first trip. For John, that was more than enough reason to partake. For Paul, it was a scary proposition, like being lost and never finding your way home again.

During a recording session for *Sgt. Pepper*, John ingested acid by mistake and became visibly ill. The straitlaced George Martin suggested he get some air and took John to the roof of their recording studio, where Lennon came close to the edge and marveled at the stars. The other Beatles realized the danger, collected their bandmate and canceled the rest of the workday. Since Paul lived within walking distance, he brought John to his house and decided to take LSD with him in the hope of reenforcing their bond[72].

---

[72] This wasn't Paul's first time with the drug, but he was still comparatively inexperienced.

Months later, a television crew asked Paul directly if he'd taken the drug, and he admitted to it. When the media shamed him for his answer, he flipped the responsibility onto them by saying he was just giving an honest response to an unsolicited question. According to his logic, if the press didn't want young fans to be influenced by the Beatles' drug use, they should stop asking the Beatles about using drugs or at least not report it. John, George and Ringo plus manager Brian Epstein supported Paul during the backlash but were privately annoyed. To Ringo, it was a private matter among the band and shouldn't have been discussed without permission from the rest. To John and George, the problem was more about Paul being the one identified with psychedelic substances instead of them. He'd resisted like a good boy for so long and now was being branded by some as a trendsetter.

Paul's reaction to marijuana, on the other hand, was unambiguously enthusiastic. The first time he tried it, he frantically asked one of the band's road managers to find him a pencil so he could write down the meaning of life. When Paul found his manifesto the next day, it simply said, "There are seven levels."

If "Got to Get You Into My Life" feels uplifting, it's by design. Paul didn't write it about a person but about the highs of pot. He takes a "ride," and it helps him find "another kind of mind." It's striking, though, how the original recording still sounds so alive despite being more than 50 years removed from its original context. Tracks like "A Day in the Life" and "Lucy in the Sky With Diamonds" have a dated hallucinogenic aura around them, yet, on its face, this is just sturdy and timeless soul music. At least, it was timeless enough to land back into the U.S. Top 10 singles chart a decade later on its own merits and then again in 1978 when it was covered by Earth, Wind and Fire.

Paul's marijuana bust in 1980 killed an expensive tour of Japan before it could begin. Had the arrest never happened—and had the Japanese concerts matched the British ones from months earlier—this doobie-worshipping song would've opened every show.

"Waterfalls"

(Paul McCartney)

Artist: Paul McCartney

Year of Recording: 1979

Appears on: *McCartney II, Wingspan (Hits and History)*

Is it selfish or selfless to become irrationally obsessed with the possibility that someone you love—maybe your lover or your child—might be in danger or even dying while your back is turned? I suppose the answer depends on whether the paralyzing fear comes from our sense of responsibility for protecting that person

162

vs. a terror over how the loss would make us feel helpless and abandoned.

Paul sings about both of those nightmares on "Waterfalls." His pleas for a love that could leave him are directed at an adult (perhaps Linda, perhaps his long-deceased mother), but the perils that spook him the most, including becoming lunch for polar bears, are the kinds of freak accidents we'd associate more with careless kids. Ludicrous on paper, they can provoke panic if you already believe in the precious fragility of a happy home life.

A song with the same name was a smash for the group TLC in 1995, and of course Paul noticed. He told *The AV Club,* "[S]omebody had a hit, a few years ago, using the first line, 'Don't go jumping waterfalls/Please stick to the lake…'And then they go off into another song. It's like, 'Excuse me?[73]'"

---

[73] A 2007 interview with Robert Siegel.

"Take It Away"

(Paul McCartney)

Artist: Paul McCartney

Year of Recording: 1981

Appears on: *Tug of War, Wingspan (Hits and History)*

Paul originally rehearsed the songs for the *Tug of War* album with Wings. But once he reteamed with Beatles producer George Martin for the actual sessions, the illusion of a democratic band seemed sillier by the minute. If you're Paul McCartney and want something to sound like Stevie Wonder, why not just call Stevie Wonder? If you're Paul McCartney and have a jazz bass part that you can't play, forget recreating it on a synthesizer. Use your clout and hire the best jazz bassist available. The Martin connection plus the philosophy of "You're Paul McCartney, dammit!" likely also helps explain the return of Ringo on most of the drums.

The revised standards and approach to personnel gave the album the shiniest polish of Paul's career regardless of one's opinion of the songwriting. Case in point is the third single, "Take It Away." The brass. The piano. And especially the flauntingly majestic "Ahhhhhh" harmony at 3:18 and onward from Linda and new recruit Eric Stewart.

It's all as meticulous as it should be for someone of Paul's stature. He'd be a solo artist from then on, with fewer and fewer instances of self-imposed false modesty.

"I'm Down"

(John Lennon-Paul McCartney)

Artist: The Beatles

Year of Recording: 1965

Appears on: *Past Masters: Volume 1*

As evidence of Paul's versatility on vocals, consider that the quietly melancholy "Yesterday," the folky and gleeful "I've Just Seen a Face" and the downright screamer "I'm Down" were all recorded on the same day. Since his teenage years and even during his first extended meeting with John Lennon, Paul used his impersonation of Little Richard like a go-to party trick, proof that the angelic-looking kid could steal the show without relying on just his pretty face. Whereas the Beatles stuck to a truncated version of "Twist and Shout" in concert to preserve John's voice, they closed nearly every performance with Paul's full "woo" routine, usually via "Long Tall Sally" and sometimes their version of Richard's medley "Kansas City/Hey, Hey, Hey."

Little Richard wasn't shy about claiming he (not Elvis) was the real king of rock and roll, and Paul has always been quick to give him deferential credit when asked about musical influences. "I'm Down" was a deliberate attempt to write his own Little Richard song and give the band a new finale to replace the aforementioned covers. Besides the frantic singing, it stands next to "Tutti Frutti," "Good Golly Miss Molly" and the rest by way of sexual frustration. Circa 1965, Mick Jagger might have been a bit jaded on account of not getting any satisfaction. An animalistic Paul, on the other hand, keeps being ordered to keep his hands to himself and is about to burst.

Between early takes of "I'm Down" released on the *Anthology* series, Paul plants the seed for an album title and dismisses Jagger as "plastic soul, man, plastic soul[74]." In other words, those Rolling Stones are all image and no feeling. Here's how you do it.

---

[74] Paul claims he wasn't using the term directly, just repeating what black musicians in America had said about Jagger's version of their style.

"Try Not to Cry"

(Paul McCartney)

Artist: Paul McCartney

Year of Recording: 1999

Appears on: *Run Devil Run*

A year after Linda's death, Paul eased his way back into business by leaning on the music that had brought him so much joy as a teenager. *Run Devil Run* is mostly 1950s oldies, and you can hear him using those songs as opportunities for self-care, either by hoping to lose himself in the energy of early rock (Elvis's "I Got Stung") or by taking an otherwise innocuous ballad for young lovers (Ricky Nelson's "Lonesome Town") and making it a platform for his deep, adult mourning.

An otherwise prolific composer, Paul only took three of the 15 slots on the album for his own material. "Try Not to Cry" represents his debut to the world as a widower, and while its simplicity fits stylistically next to the cover tunes, naked vulnerability can't hide behind a genre exercise. Paul woke up in the morning, and his goal here, after losing his closest companion of 30 years, has nothing to do with his usual eagerness to please an audience and everything to do with making it through the damn day. He likes to sing, he acknowledges, and he'll do it. But he knows it's a fake-it-till-you-make-it distraction. In the emergency of the moment, he still needs someone—likely Linda's spirit, if she's out there—to stabilize his wounds.

"Heather"

(Paul McCartney)

Artist: Paul McCartney

Year of Recording: 2001

Appears on: *Driving Rain*

Paul was never perceived by the British press as the cool Beatle, at least not while all the others were alive. Even eventual biographer Philip Norman once used newspaper space in the 1970s for a cruelly mocking poem that read in part, ""O deified Scouse, with unmusical spouse/For the cliches and cloy you unload/To an anodyne tune may they bury you soon/In the middlemost midst of the road." And though he would grumble in private, the public version of Paul kept smiling and pointing both thumbs in the air, an attitude that only added to his image as a bit of a square.

All the decades of decent PR instincts likely paid off during Paul's messy divorce from Heather Mills. The newspapers (and Norman, too) dug into the details revealed by insiders and court documents and sided sympathetically with the guy who was always willing to put on a happy face for the cameras and tell the origin story behind "Yesterday" for the zillionth time. As for Heather, Britain's polarizing *Sun* tabloid called her a "Hooker, Liar, Porn Star, Fantasist, Trouble Maker, Shoplifter" and double-dog-dared her to bring a libel suit.

At various points in her life, Heather claimed to have been sexually abused by a kidnapper, grown up with a physically abusive father, been forced into shoplifting and to have spent months living homeless in a cardboard box. That's all on top of indisputably being hit by a motorcycle and losing a leg. Many have questioned her relationship with the truth, some have defended her, and not enough (in my opinion) have considered a nuanced third option: That parts of her story may have been amplified for dramatic impact but that they come from a real life of authentic anger and pain regardless of the details.

Paul already had nearly 40 years of extreme fame under his belt when he met Heather, long enough to spot and shoo away the obviously opportunistic bullshitters. It had been him, alone among the Beatles, who had rejected the ethically challenged Allen Klein as a business manager, so sure of smelling a rat that he sued his three best friends in order to be freed from him.

No matter his thoughts on his ex-wife today, Paul saw something in her that brought him back to life and reintroduced him to feelings that must've felt a lot like love back then. The song "Heather" is what played as the bride walked down the aisle at their wedding.

"Come and Get It"

(John Lennon-Paul McCartney)

Artist: The Beatles

Year of Recording: 1969

Appears on: *Anthology 3*

After the death of Brian Epstein, the Beatles poured their money into their own business, Apple Corp., with Paul supposedly responsible for the title pun and the art direction for the entity's logo. It was a disastrous overreach that poisoned their relationships with one another for at least the remainder of John Lennon's life. What was a rock band doing, anyway, running a fashion boutique or collecting patents on consumer electronics? But when its creators kept Apple strictly in the music business as a record label, the results weren't bad at all. Along with John, Paul, George and Ringo, Apple's roster of artists included an early version of Hot Chocolate, a young James Taylor (ultimately produced and managed by Paul's near-brother-in-law Peter Asher) and Beatle pal Billy Preston.

The biggest and most frustrating legacy of Apple Records, though, belongs to Badfinger. They'd been discovered by Beatles roadie Mal Evans as the Iveys and were renamed after the original title of the *Sgt. Pepper* track "A Little Help From My Friends" (initially known as "Bad Finger Boogie"). They had a great songwriter of their own in Pete Ham, but their first big hit came from Paul, who gave them "Come and Get It" under one condition: Copy my demo and don't dare change a thing.

Absent the addition of some harmonies and a slightly quicker tempo, they followed orders and built on the initial success. "Day After Day" (produced by George), "Baby Blue" (which plays out the final scene in *Breaking Bad*), "Without You" (a smash when covered by both Harry Nilsson and Mariah Carey) and "No Matter What" are all timelessly classic rock and, dare I say it, even better than the poppy yet slightly underwritten gift Paul had given them.

Burdened by financial problems, Ham hung himself in 1975, and Tom Evans—who Paul picked for lead vocals on "Come and Get It"—did the same in 1983.

"Great Day"

(Paul McCartney)

Artist: Paul McCartney

Year of Recording: 1992

Appears on: *Flaming Pie, Pure McCartney*

Paul tacked "Great Day" onto the end of *Flaming Pie* to lighten the mood and send listeners home with a relaxed grin. He and Linda had sung it to their kids for 20 years and probably perfected a tight double act around the house. Though she'd moved much further into the background on her husband's records by then, Linda's harmonies are a reminder of the couple's *Ram*, the best example of Paul the arranger finding a blend between himself and a spouse who never claimed to be a vocalist. Linda had come into Paul's circle by being the rare female rock-and-roll photographer back in the '60s, but she never wanted to be behind the keyboards, shaking a tambourine and cheering her partner's fans on. She was always there simply because Paul wanted/needed her there.

Out of what was released during her lifetime, this was Linda's last contribution to one of Paul's songs.

"Paperback Writer"

(John Lennon-Paul McCartney)

Artist: The Beatles

Year of Recording: 1966

Appears on: *Past Masters: Volume 2, 1962-1966, 1*

Paired with "Rain" as my favorite A-side/B-side single of all time, "Paperback Writer" isn't much on the page. The song is built around just two easy guitar chords (C and G), and the lyrics are a poor-man's Kinks character study, missing the wit and detail typical of Ray Davies. But, oh, the sound!

Until then, Paul's bass was barely audible on the Beatles' records, so he switched from his usual Hofner violin-shaped model to a Rickenbacker, which he'd utilize for the next 20 years. Then he took even fewer chances of not being heard by pumping each note from his new toy through a loudspeaker. From then on, he'd be mentioned as one of the most melodic of bassists in popular music, second only perhaps to Motown session man James Jamerson.

That's him, too, adding to the heaviness on lead guitar. Meanwhile, as pointed out by the late critic Ian

MacDonald, George and John are indeed singing "Frere Jacques" as backup during one of the verses[75].

"Lady Madonna" (Take 2)

(John Lennon-Paul McCartney)

Artist: The Beatles

Year of Recording: 1968

Appears on: *The Beatles (2018 Super Deluxe* reissue only)

Paul's mother worked as a nurse, a community-revered job that helped the working-class family earn a middle-class home from the government, including their street's only phone. A dutiful Mary McCartney would spring into action at all hours of the day, pedaling a bike in snowy winter months as best she could, usually on her way to deliver a baby.

The initial influence on "Lady Madonna," though, came from a January 1965 photo in *National Geographic* of a topless Vietnamese woman with a child feeding from her breast. These days, Paul champions the song as a tribute to all women, but no one would blame him for playing it so often merely as an excuse to boogie on the piano like Fats Domino, who did his own version in the same year of release. As uneasy as he felt trotting

---

[75] See *Revolution in the Head.*

out Beatles songs early in his solo career, he chose this happy tune as the first from his old band to make it into a Wings setlist, five years after the breakup.

On this take, it's just Paul on piano and Ringo playing drums (with brushes in place of sticks). But even without any emphasis on vocals—as a dear friend pointed out to me—it's almost impossible not to add your own "see how they run" at all the right spots.

"How Kind of You"

(Paul McCartney)

Artist: Paul McCartney

Year of Recording: 2005

Appears on: *Chaos and Creation in the Backyard*

When a 60-something Paul asked George Martin to name a producer he should work with, Martin steered him toward Nigel Godrich, most famous for overseeing projects by Radiohead and Beck. At first, the songs they did together included Paul's touring band, but Godrich got the other musicians out of the picture and forced Paul to make most of *Chaos and Creation in the Backyard* nearly one on one. He was also adamant about the songs Paul brought in and dismissed a share of them as not good enough. The two would argue on occasion, and Paul took a breather from the sessions by teaming with a different and more easygoing producer (David Kahne) for part of what would be released a few years later as *Memory Almost Full*. But then Paul came back to Godrich and finished the project that would ultimately net him a late-career Grammy nomination for Album of the Year.

Regardless of whether the discipline was imposed by Godrich or coincidence, *Chaos* is the rare McCartney collection with a consistent, all-of-a-piece sound and tone. I was shocked at how much I disliked it upon first listen way back in my simple-minded twenties. There's little feel-good pop on it from a musician who does feel-good pop better than anyone, and the idea of recording Paul mainly by himself didn't result in the wacky experimentation that dominates, say, "Temporary Secretary" or any of the other tracks on *McCartney II*. The material is measured and mature, from an adult who'd been handling a series of complex emotions in a short span and could compartmentalize them via skills that would be lost on a younger man. It's not a breakup album but rather an unofficial narrative of a full, meaningful, mixed-bag of a relationship. Paul finds a romantic savior ("How Kind of You"), yearns to build upon an intimate connection ("Friends to Go"), and accepts that the best things about the person he loves don't come without a set of problems ("Too Much Rain"). Then there's bitter disappointment ("Riding to Vanity Fair"), the potential for renewed commitment ("Promise to You Girl") and the supportive strength to push forward ("Follow

176

Me"). Ahead with the same person? With someone else? With friends and family in the meantime? Take your pick.

Chaos is the first and thus far only McCartney album that gets replayed not because of anything catchy but because of everything Paul says in his lyrics. His feelings are so naked, and yet he's somehow so calm about them, too. Had he ever wanted to tour behind a record in small theaters with just a piano and some self-effacing assistance from a drummer and a guitarist, this would've been the obvious chance.

"Magneto and Titanium Man" (Live Version)

(Paul McCartney-Linda McCartney)

Artist: Wings

Year of Recording: 1976

Appears on: *Wings Over America*

Long before calling Her Majesty "a pretty nice girl" during the final seconds of *Abbey Road*, Paul wrote an essay about Queen Elizabeth II upon her taking the throne. Among all others in his 10-year-old age group, Paul's entry was deemed the best in Liverpool and earned him a gift certificate for a free book from the city's mayor. Young John Lennon probably would've used the prize to snare something by Lewis Carroll or another example of sly wordplay. Paul, though, went for a book on modern art.

Depending on who you ask, comic books would qualify as art, and Paul would agree. He missed out on the golden age of Marvel/DC as a kid but got into them while traveling around the United States with his kids in the 1970s. This explains "Magneto and Titanium Man," which played during Wings' 1975-1976 world tour with characters from Jack Kirby displayed in the background. Paul opted for less pop art and a more conventionally tasteful style when he published his own collection of paintings in 1999.

The live version referenced here comes from *Wings Over America*, a full setlist from the 1976 concerts. Back when record stores stocked bootlegs under the wink-wink title of "Dutch imports," a pirated copy of an L.A. show sold too well to be ignored. Originally planned as a two-album set, the official release had a third piece of vinyl added in an effort to kill the competition from the black market.

"The Ballad of the Skeletons"

(Allen Ginsberg-Paul McCartney-Philip Glass)

Artist: Allen Ginsberg, Paul McCartney, Philip Glass and Lenny Kaye

Year of Recording: 1995

Appears on: *Flaming Pie (Archive Collection* only*)*

Before forming his professional and sexual partnership with Yoko Ono, John Lennon dismissed the avant garde as "French for bullshit." Paul was more open to experimental art up to that point, partly due to a personal interest and because he kept his home in London near a culturally engaged crowd instead of relocating to the quieter suburbs.

In some accounts, Paul met Yoko before John did, evidence of his proximity to the scene compared to the other Beatles. Depending on who's telling the story and when, Yoko approached Paul behind the guise of wanting copies of old lyrics as a birthday gift for composer John Cage. (If true, the story contradicts Yoko's fervent claims that she didn't know who the Beatles were prior to meeting Lennon, quite a stretch for a conceptual artist living in London in the mid-1960s.) The anecdote ends with Paul claiming to not have anything around the house and shooing Yoko away but suggesting she contact John instead.

The official narrative has John and Yoko meeting in November 1966 at an exhibition at the Indica Gallery. The Indica's owners included Paul's friend and future biographer Barry Miles plus Peter Asher, the brother of Paul's then girlfriend. For a while, the Indica doubled as a bookstore, and Paul met a series of famous scribes as a result of his connections. One among many was poet Allen Ginsberg. Roughly a year before Ginsberg died, Paul backed him up by playing most of the instruments on "The Ballad of the Skeletons." Lenny Kaye of the Patti Smith Group did the bass and took the producer's chair. Phillip Glass was on piano.

"Flaming Pie"

(Paul McCartney)

Artist: Paul McCartney

Year of Recording: 1996

Appears on: *Flaming Pie*

If some combination of the Elvis Costello pairing plus the 1989/1990 tour prompted Paul to finally dip both feet into his Beatle past, his participation in *The Beatles Anthology* project was his chance to soak his whole body in it. Without John Lennon around to counter his own version of the narrative, Paul became comfortable asserting his slant on the band's story without deferring instinctively to the other players. In individual interviews filmed for the television production, George and Ringo each speak in semi-casual environments, maybe behind a mixing console at a recording studio or outdoors at home. Paul, meanwhile, goes for the drama and is taped during a break at a large-venue soundcheck, in front of a campfire or, best of all, while steering a tugboat. His settings stand out, as if they'll add weight to his words when/if he's contradicted by what the other two participants might say. Besides the promos for the two reunion songs debuted on the show, the images you remember most from the program are of him, shaping the group's history with a tight hold.

George Harrison sometimes accused Paul of hinting conveniently at a Beatles reunion whenever he had a new solo album to promote. In the case of *Flaming Pie*, it nearly worked. Paul had Ringo on drums for a few tracks and brought back George Martin to arrange some orchestration. He supposedly did the title song in four hours, in tribute to how quickly the Beatles could polish off a new tune rather than tinker until everything went stale.

Even the title, "Flaming Pie," was a Fab tie-in, a reference to how John once told the press that the name "Beatles" with an "A" was brought down to him by a spaceman from a flying saucer/burning dessert. Of course, John was gone by then, and Paul could insert himself firmly into the tall tale as the star. From this point forward, he was the man on the flaming pie, the one now responsible—self-appointed or otherwise—for maintaining the band's stature, magic and mystique.

In the meantime, though, his record company told him to keep his own music to himself for a while. There were plenty of *Anthology* CDs in stores, and better to get the most out of those sales and not confuse the market with extra product. Minus an overdub or two, the album was ready to go roughly three months after *Anthology* aired, but it would sit unreleased for another year.

"Ever Present Past"

(Paul McCartney)

Artist: Paul McCartney

Year of Recording: 2006

Appears on: *Memory Almost Full*

Contrary what he sang as a Beatle, Paul hadn't lost much hair by the time he was 64 and didn't require anyone to feed him. Instead, he was still a star, still touring and still making big news, such as by becoming the first major artist signed to the Starbucks record label, Hear Music. What blasted out of each coffee shop, though, (likely on a loop that drove every barista nuts) were fittingly the thoughts of an older man taking stock of where he'd been and what he'd become.

Whereas the looking-back contemplation and tone of *Flaming Pie* had been slanted largely toward his former band, the appropriately titled *Memory Almost Full* was a more personal retrospective. Paul used it to recollect his time at school, his teenage insecurity, his rise to fame, and how all the money in the world hadn't shielded him from excruciating tragedy. Near the end, he even bravely imagined his own death and left friends and fandom with a request for jokes to be told at his wake.

"Ever Present Past" comes early in the track listing and lets us know that these songs won't be blind, feel-good nostalgia trips. They're chances for Paul to reevaluate his life choices, aided as they were from time to time by a little luck. He'd recounted so many stories in countless interviews by this point, and some of the biggest moments might not have seemed real anymore, too distant to touch and too warped by rock-and-roll myth to trust. Revisiting it all, he essentially wonders if his own story is true and whether it all actually happened to him. He concludes affirmatively, with equal parts pride and astonishment, "The things I think I did? I D-I-D did." In other words, "I'm Paul (bleeping) McCartney!" Mic drop.

"We Can Work It Out"

(John Lennon-Paul McCartney)

Artist: The Beatles

Year of Recording: 1965

Appears on: *Past Masters: Volume 2, 1962-1966, 1*

Despite being notably attentive to his first few girlfriends, Paul was also controlling during those early romances. In at least two cases, for example (Dot Rhone and Iris Caldwell), Paul dictated how his partners should wear their hair and dress. He took after John in that regard, and both men pushed their dates to look as much like blonde French movie star Brigitte Bardot as possible.

A successful actress long before she'd ever met Paul, Jane Asher kept her red hair and wasn't as inclined to give up her own life for the sake of a mate. Rather than wait at home for Paul's return from worldwide touring, she continued building her own career and was often performing in a play when he'd be free from his own obligations. They stayed together for five years and nearly married but were still so young when it was over (26 for him, 22 for her). And for all his natural charm, Paul's immature unwillingness to compromise is suggested within several of his Asher-influenced songs from that youthful period.

Don't be fooled by the diplomatic title of "We Can Work It Out" or its composer's cheery delivery of the lead vocal. Paul's lyrics for it are a my-way-or-the-highway threat. He pleads with his combatant to "see it my way" without ever agreeing to shift his own perspective, and he'll keep up with his demands by "talking until [he]he can't go on." If his lover won't budge, well, there's "the risk of knowing that [their] love may soon be gone" or that it'll "fall apart." With angry condescension, he dismisses what the other person is thinking and asks her to consider how "you can get it wrong and still you think that it's all right." Silly girl.

Even the contemplative bridge section about life being too short for "fussing and fighting" is just a temperature-lowering tactic to get what he wants. There's no peace offering after it. Instead, we get the unyielding "So I will ask you once again...Try to see it my way." Put simply, we can work it out, as long as you do what I say.

Paul would evolve by marrying an independent woman who was nonetheless willing to stay nearly literally by his side while he played the role of rock star. Within a few years of moving on, Jane would meet cartoonist Gerald Scarfe, who'd forge his own connection to the music business by designing stage and album artwork for Pink Floyd (most prominently for *The Wall*).

"Helter Skelter"

(John Lennon-Paul McCartney)

Artist: The Beatles

Year of Recording: 1968

Appears on: *The Beatles*

Chapter 9 of the Book of Revelation mentions locusts, four angels, a bottomless pit, and men with hair like women. To Charles Manson, nearly all of those things were the Beatles, and the songs on the band's self-titled "white" album were prophetic orders for him and his followers to initiate a holocaust-like race war. Manson believed he'd create songs that would attract white women into his cult, thereby depriving black men of supposed sexual outlets and provoking a killing spree in which at least one-third of the white population would die. In the meantime, Manson and company would hide underground (the previously mentioned bottomless pit) until the time was right to reemerge and overpower the black survivors.

For Manson, it was all there in the music, not to mention the color of the album sleeve. John Lennon was singing "Revolution" and telling people, "We'd all love to see the plan." George Harrison was writing "Piggies," a song taken by murderous listeners as orders to bring down the establishment. The sound collage "Revolution 9" kept repeating the phrase "number nine" second after second, reminding Manson of the specific chapter in the most apocalyptic of biblical books. And then there was Paul McCartney, who Manson assumed was provoking the African-American community with a tune called "Blackbird," in which the listener is told this is the "moment to arise."

It was Paul, too, who came up with "Helter Skelter," a deliberate attempt to make the loudest, dirtiest rock-and-roll record in history after the Who's Pete Townshend had congratulated himself for doing just that with "I Can See for Miles." Like the British slide that shares its name, it was intended by Paul as a musical depiction of a twisted drop to the bottom. To biographer Barry Miles, he compared it to "the rise and fall of the Roman Empire...the fall, the demise, the going down." Manson heard it as the soundtrack to the coming carnage.

The most famous of Manson's victims, actress Sharon Tate, likely wasn't a target. Unfortunately, she'd been staying at the same house once rented by record producer Terry Melcher. Manson knew Melcher through a member of the Beach Boys and had gotten the impression that Melcher would help him get a record deal, something that he hoped would've exposed his work to all the hippy white girls in San Francisco and led them to him. Either Manson was looking for Melcher or at least used the same house to send the scariest of messages. At another site, Manson's people killed two others and wrote "Pigs" on the wall and "Healter Skelter" (sic) on the refrigerator in their victims' blood. Back in England, the only harm even remotely intended by the song involved the painful blisters on Ringo Starr's fingers, the byproduct of playing the drums so fiercely.

"Things We Said Today"

(John Lennon-Paul McCartney)

Artist: The Beatles

Year of Recording: 1964

Appears on: *A Hard Day's Night*

Though rejected both as a single and as part of their first film, "Things We Said Today" was a favorite among the Beatles, including the hard-to-impress John Lennon. If Paul hadn't taken the lead vocals, it could've been confused easily as John's song. The minor chords in the verses give it a darker mystique than Paul's usual ballads from the early 1960s. And while the couple in the lyrics might be in love for now, the narrative takes some ominous turns that suggest this paradise of romance is short-lived.

Like Paul and his then-girlfriend Jane Asher, the characters expect to be kept apart, maybe by their globetrotting careers or their independent growth in competing directions. The idyllic scene, while appreciated in the moment, is simultaneously already being earmarked as a memory that the two of them will recall in their saddest moments. No wonder "Can't Buy Me Love" was deemed the more commercial option for the movie and the charts.

"Press"

(Paul McCartney)

Artist: Paul McCartney

Year of Recording: 1985

Appears on: *Press to Play*

To test your tolerance/giddiness for Paul after these many pages of half-baked verbosity, take a listen to "Press," specifically via its 1986 promo video. A middle-aged man with a mighty mullet enters happily into a crowded subway, wearing a collared, short-sleeved shirt and khakis. His first words after counting the song in are "Darling, I love you very, very, very much." You still with me, adverbs or otherwise?

So, he gets inside a train car, yearning for Darling's touch but too embarrassed to admit any horniness in such a tight, public space. If only the two of them could role-play their way into a secret word to sustain the sexual tension until they reach their stop. But is this about Paul and Linda or maybe some stand-in for Paul's wife who he's eying from his seat?

Yeah, not so much. He raises his eyebrows, smiles and points his fingers into "hey, how's it goin'" guns at EVERYONE in his sightline and then transfers to another route so he can sing to and get kisses from a fresh set of passengers. They're all things you'd want from some unaccompanied dude during your rush-hour commute. Mind you, again, this is all happening while he's communicating on the subject of risqué release. Just tell Paul to "press," and he's game.

You watch, and your jaw has dropped too low, and your mouth is too wide open with shock to laugh at Dad embarrassing himself so much in front of all your friends. That is, unless you've learned to love McCartney by now. In the latter case, the eyes quit rolling after the first minute and then you're right there with those extras in their seats, imagining how awesome it would be to have Paul climb aboard at your station and chat everyone up. Smiles, winks, autographs. thumbs in the air and, yes, singing and kissing (for those who request it, anyway).

A few years ago, Paul went viral through his "Carpool Karaoke" segment on *The Late Late Show With James Corden* (26 million-plus YouTube views as of this writing). The clip ends with random customers at a Liverpool pub hearing the opening chord to "A Hard Day's Night'" and realizing "Holy sh$%! It's HIM!"

Like for those on the "Press" shoot, how's that for an afternoon?

"The Pound Is Sinking"

(Paul McCartney)

Artist: Paul McCartney

Year of Recording: 1981

Appears on: *Tug of War*

Besides offering one of the few instances of noticeable electric guitar on the hugely successful *Tug of War*, "The Pound Is Sinking" sticks out to me for its strange combination of segments rolled into a single song. Paul has combined various bits many times, but the ones merged here are more of an odd hodgepodge than usual. Most of the lyrics mock anxieties over currency, and then there's a wife belittling her husband, claiming he's nothing like his father. But the standout section that could've/should've been its own fleshed-out track comes in at about 1:50. There's flat denial of a serious matter, followed by the suggestion that if it DID occur, it lasted for just a second.

The narrator tries to double-down on that defense, but he goes so quickly from casual to shrieking, as if the charges, regardless of their truth, were triggering hurtful memories for the accused. And if we decide it's still the same person talking, there's an intriguing counter-attack. Maybe it COULD'VE happened, but "your heart just wasn't in it." In other words, we had a chance at a history, more than a moment, and you—not me—were the one who blew it.

In the early '80s, Paul took a paternity test in response to allegations of fathering a German daughter while the pre-fame Beatles were in residence at a Hamburg club. He admitted to knowing the mother, and some money was provided in the mid-'60s to keep the story out of the papers. After it came back—this time with a much larger price tag for silence—Paul gave some blood samples that indicated he wasn't the father. Mother and daughter alleged that the analyzed specimen came from an impostor, so he submitted more blood and got the case dismissed by the courts. Paying the legal bills for both sides didn't calm the situation, and he'd need to react to the same accusers for years.

So, maybe the song means something. Or maybe, as Paul has deemed it, it's just one of those "jumbles of words" prompted, who knows why, by the subconscious.

"You Know My Name (Look Up the Number)"

(John Lennon-Paul McCartney)

Artist: The Beatles

Year of Recording: 1967 and 1969

Appears on: *Past Masters: Volume 2*

John Lennon got the original idea for "You Know My Name (Look Up the Number)" from staring at a phone book. It was intended at first as a mantra-like chant (seven, sometimes 15 minutes of the title phrase sung again and again) but evolved into a wacky comedy record. The Beatles worked on it over four different sessions spanning roughly three years, including a guest spot from Brian Jones of the Rolling Stones on saxophone.

After screaming along with John at the start, Paul is introduced as "Dennis O' Bell" and morphs into a lounge singer. The parody paid tribute to Denis O'Dell, who ran the band's film division and concluded a respectable cinematic career by helping manage the initially infamous but since reappraised Michael Cimino movie *Heaven's Gate*. Thanks to the song, O'Dell constantly received calls at home from fans, as if he'd actually invited them to look up his number and make contact. Here's betting his family was very pleased, particularly in their most sleep-deprived moments.

Whereas the basic track was laid down around the time of *Magical Mystery Tour* (when domestic life among the band was still tranquil), the vocals were added in 1969 by John and Paul at a time when tensions were high. The fact that they could still share a microphone in those days and clearly make each other laugh is likely a reassuring memory for Paul regarding such a complicated friendship with a since-deceased partner. Out of everything that he, John, George and Ringo made together, the man who wrote "Yesterday," "Let It Be" and "Hey Jude" has named this as his favorite Beatles recording[76].

"Deliver Your Children"

(Paul McCartney-Denny Laine)

Artist: Wings

Year of Recording: 1977

Appears on: *London Town*

"This is for all the Wings fans!" Paul proclaimed when dusting off the song "Too Many People" in concert circa 2005. The thing is, though, it was a deep cut from

---

[76] Mentioned in Paul's interview as part of Mark Lewisohn's *The Beatles: Recording Sessions.*

his and Linda's album *Ram* and not on anything credited to his stadium-filing second band. For all the retrospective warmth he's learned to express toward the Beatles, Paul still hasn't fully embraced Wings. The latter group actually recorded longer than the Beatles and had 15 Top 10 singles and eight Top 10 albums in less than a decade in the United States. Gosh, what an embarrassment.

Unlike most of his more modern records, Paul didn't record those songs mostly alone. Wings had eight other members over the course of five different lineups. Linda sang harmonies and played keyboards during their entire run, but the only other musician who got in at the beginning and lasted until the end was guitarist/vocalist Denny Laine. Paul knew Denny from the early days of the Moody Blues and brought him on as sort of the highest ranking of sidemen. Denny would recruit new players after someone's resignation, get to sing three or so songs in concert and maybe snag a track on an album, sometimes one of his own, sometimes one written by Paul.

Denny's contributions are heard most audibly on *London Town*. Out of its 14 cuts, five were co-writes between him and Paul. Whereas Paul's songs from that period have a safe pop sensibility, his work with Denny comes across as more folky in spots (as is the case with "Deliver Your Children") and more experimental in others. And although it didn't make the album, their

"Mull of Kintyre" was a smash in England, the first single in the United Kingdom to sell two million copies.

The last iteration of Wings had Denny back to his one-vocal-per-album duties. He and Paul would work together for a few more years, but their relationship soured after Paul's marijuana bust jettisoned an expectedly profitable tour of Japan. Following some financial troubles, Denny sold gossipy stories to the press and cozied up to a biographer who was hungry for dirt on Paul and Linda. When the hour-and-a-half documentary *Wingspan* was shown on national television, touting Paul's successes in the 1970s, Denny's name was mentioned exactly once.

"Listen to What the Man Said"

(Paul McCartney-Linda McCartney)

Artist: Wings

Year of Recording: 1975

Appears on: *Venus and Mars, All the Best, Wingspan (Hits and History), Pure McCartney*

There's not much to "Listen to What the Man Said," not even a verse after the first minute. Still, after some labored attempts to determine what was missing, Paul and Wings compiled all the pieces necessary to build one of the most joyous of pop records. Made in New

Orleans, it opens with Paul doing a cheeky impression of Meters lead guitarist Leo Nocentelli ("Yeh, yeh."). Linda, too, got into a playful mood and contributed the smooching effect heard after a line about a kiss.

The star of the track, though, is sax player Tom Scott, who'd likely shrug his shoulders at such a compliment. Scott participated in a near fluke by happening to live close to the session and getting an out-of-the-blue invitation to stop by. Not unlike other horn players who've worked on Paul's solo albums, he didn't intend for what we now hear to make it into the final version and was just warming up with a first pass. (See also Howie Casey's guest appearance on 1973's "Bluebird.") Paul humored Scott by letting him do a few more official takes, but the fresh and peppy energy of those initial notes—with hardly any understanding that the tape was rolling—were more than enough to please the boss. The same perfectionist who reportedly annoyed the other Beatles by ordering 60 or so tries at "Ob-La-Di, Ob-La-Da"—a composition he admitted to not liking much in the first place—must've been kidnapped and replaced in the interim.

"Get Back"

(John Lennon-Paul McCartney)

Artist: The Beatles

Year of Recording: 1969

Appears on: *Let It Be, 1967-1970, Past Masters: Volume 2* and *1*

Early versions of "Get Back" included satirical digs at British politician Enoch Powell, who'd vehemently opposed legislation that prohibited housing discrimination against immigrants (among other protections). Paul intended lines like "Don't want no Pakistanis stealing other people's jobs" as mockery but reasoned that the message would've been lost in translation, with his anti-racist comments being seen as just the opposite. John Lennon, meanwhile, assumed the song was about Paul's reaction to Yoko Ono but participated when given the rare opportunity to play the song's slide-guitar solo instead of his usual role on rhythm.

In its final form, the record likely has no message and served primarily as an excuse for the tense personal feelings among the band to be set aside in favor of a fun, bluesy jam. Hoping the group would be on its best behavior in the presence of a guest, George Harrison brought pianist Billy Preston to the sessions and gave him a prominent cameo in the instrumentation. The label on the single for "Get Back" was credited to "The Beatles With Billy Preston," the only time the lads from Liverpool gave such a publicly acknowledged nod to another musician on one of their own releases.

Prior to breaking up, the Beatles at least flirted with the idea of becoming a loose, collective unit, maybe with people like Preston serving as a member here and there and with on-and-off contributions from each of the four core leaders. As much as he likely would've accepted other ways of keeping everyone together, Paul allegedly brushed the proposal aside, perhaps fearing it would be John's way of bringing Yoko into the act on an official basis.

"Get Back" was performed multiple times at the Beatles' iconic rooftop concert to finish the *Let It Be* project. Audio from the last attempt, before police pulled the plug on the noise, famously included the Lennon witticism about hoping the band had passed their audition. The same take includes Paul saying, "Thanks, Mo," in reference to Ringo Starr's first wife and her enthusiastic response within the tiny crowd. When she died of a brain tumor some 20 years later, Paul penned "Little Willow" (released on *Flaming Pie*) as a tribute.

"I Love This House"

(Paul McCartney)

Artist: Paul McCartney

Year of Recording: 1984 and 1985

Appears on: *Flaming Pie (Archive Collection* only*)*

When Paul and his brother, Mike, were kids, their father rigged up a set of headphones that ran from the family's living room up to each boy's bedroom, allowing for a listen to rare rock-and-roll broadcasts on late-night radio even after being tucked in. Paul inherited his father's handiness and put it to good use when he and Linda moved into a bare Scottish farmhouse. At first, they had no hot water and got by on furniture made from old crates. The living conditions improved as children were born, but the McCartneys remained a relatively unfussy, unpretentious and low-maintenance family. Money was spent on fancy holidays. Home was a few-frills place for parents, kids, loads of pets and lasting memories.

The years 1985 through 1989 were packed with songs that Paul either never released or sat on for an extended time and ultimately relegated to B-sides on obscure CD singles. The reason may have been twofold. Mainly, Paul had splurged on a home recording studio by then and could indulge his workaholic tendencies on his own schedule on a whim without needing to prioritize his prime material. That period, though, was also the closest he would ever come to commercial insignificance. *Give My Regards to Broad Street* had been a critical and box-office bomb, and *Press to Play* updated his sound while baffling his fanbase, becoming the lowest-charting official studio album of his career. The baby boomers had grown up and were ready to embrace 1960s memories—the 20th anniversary of the Beatles' *Sgt. Pepper* and the so-called "Summer of Love" came with considerable media hype in 1987—but the business-conscious Paul stayed fairly quiet. He kept making music but seemed to be holding himself to a higher standard than usual, maybe worried about the long-term impact of a third-straight non-seller.

As bootleggers have proven, there was more than enough material to fill out a full album and cash in. Much of it got lumped together into what hardcore followers refer to as the *Return to Pepperland* sessions. Most famously associated with producer Phil Ramone and parts of Billy Joel's band, a lot actually features different personnel. In the case of "I Love This House," Paul was joined by Pink Floyd's David Gilmour on guitar, Fairport Convention's Dave Mattacks on drums and producer David Foster (not Ramone) on keyboards. It stayed in the can for a dozen years.

"Back on My Feet"

(Paul McCartney-Declan MacManus)

Artist: Paul McCartney

Year of Recording: 1987

Appears on: *Flowers in the Dirt (Archive Collection* only*)*

"Back on My Feet" makes sense as the first stab at collaboration between Paul and Elvis Costello. Its dry and inauthentic production values are in line with a period in the McCartney catalog when its maker seemed timid in his creativity and uncertain of his musical relevancy. Lyrically, though, it isn't the least bit sleepy, focusing on a character who insists he's still a force to be reckoned with despite being dismissed by his neighbors as a loser. Paul's words are mostly defiant and set us up for a redemption song, but then Linda comes in near the end with Elvis's main contribution, a cynical rebuttal that mocks the poor guy for his stubborn and supposedly delusional pride. Will he ever stand up again as promised, or is he hopelessly crippled and doomed to embarrass himself by trying?

Paul might've been wondering the same about his professional prospects at the time, and he approached the marketing of this trial run with Elvis cautiously. Whereas the Costello connection became central to the public narrative for *Flowers in the Dirt* some two years later, "Back on My Feet" had a quiet debut on the

202

flipside of a holiday single. Paul would find his groove again with some help from his new writing partner. Maybe he was waiting to see if he could sustain it before inviting closer scrutiny and taking a bow.

"Too Many People" (*Thrillington* Version)

(Paul McCartney)

Artist: Percy "Thrills" Thrillington

Year of Recording: 1971

Appears on: *Thrillington*

Treated by critics as a trifle when it was released, *Ram* now qualifies among many fans as Paul's solo best. Paul's initial confidence in the material was suggested by his choice to commission an instrumental version of the whole thing in an orchestral big-band style two months after the official sessions. But once the rock-and-roll side of the project failed to catch as much fire as it deserved, the oddball vanity indulgence went into the vaults and remained there for six years.

When the instrumental recordings finally emerged, they went out under the title *Thrillington*, as in Percy "Thrills" Thrillington, a made-up conductor who had supposedly languished in obscurity until having his talents discovered by Paul and Linda. "Thrills," the story went, became renowned not for his music but for placing frequent personal ads of congratulations and best wishes in assorted British newspapers. Paul and company did exactly that in advance of the eventual release and aided the ruse. The liner notes added another layer of playful deception by being credited to a Clint Harrigan. Paul played dumb about the entire game until 1990, when he admitted that both Clint and "Thrills" were the same joker who used to play bass in the Beatles.

"Letting Go"

(Paul McCartney-Linda McCartney)

Artist: Wings

Year of Recording: 1974 and 1975

Appears on: *Venus and Mars*

Upon joining Paul in Wings, guitarist Denny Laine hoped to bring aboard American keyboardist Paul Harris, too. Harris had played with bluesman B.B. King and a then-unknown Nick Drake and would later work heavily with Stephen Stills. Without any mind to pedigree, Paul tapped his musically untrained wife for the role, in part for emotional support and to maintain the option of harmonizing with a female vocalist as needed.

Linda looks awkward in early rehearsal footage with the band, not exactly nervous but too stiffly focused on not making mistakes. A few tours later, by 1976, she'd figured out how to pose with some authority behind her instrument and at least looked the part of a big-haired glam rocker in an arena act. According to reports from other band members, though, she would've preferred to have been home with Paul and the kids and had tired of living on a stage.

"Letting Go" communicates Paul's feelings toward his supportive spouse and his molding of her into a reluctant yet hardworking colleague. She's a "brand-new star," and he wants to put her both on the radio and in a Broadway show. She'd do it all if asked, but at what cost? Having proven a willingness to please and sacrifice for her mate, shouldn't she receive the same from him at some point in return?

The couple stayed off the road for most of the 1980s. By the time they returned to face an audience again, Linda had reclaimed a career as a photographer and put out the first in a series of vegetarian-themed cookbooks.

As for the song, if you ever notice Paul in concert with a horn section, expect to find it in the setlist. Podcaster and music professor Chris Mercer found the correct adjective for it: Smoky[77].

---

[77] From the "Venus and Mars" episode of the *Take It Away* podcast.

"Monkberry Moon Delight"

(Paul McCartney-Linda McCartney)

Artist: Paul and Linda McCartney

Year of Recording: 1970 and 1971

Appears on: *Ram*

"Monkberry Moon Delight" originated as just a goofy nonsense song inspired by Paul's young daughters' mispronunciation of "milk" as "monk." From there, he gave himself a license to include the most absurd imagery he could think of, including but not limited to a pillow up his nose. He had the spooky oldies hit "Love Potion #9" in his head, and simple "monk" became the mysterious drink of the title.

In its final mad form, it's hard to hear the track and not fall into a full-blown panic attack. The lyrics, like some of our most difficult bouts with fear, aren't based in reality but don't lose their scary power in the moment.

In his comprehensive study *Paul McCartney: Recording Sessions*, author Luca Perasi connects the nightmarish tone to a quote from Paul to friend Barry Miles about his mental health immediately after the Beatles' breakup (and right around the time of the song's creation). "I was going through a bad time, what I suspect was a nervous breakdown. I remember lying awake at nights shaking."

Paul's manic howler of a vocal caught the ears of Screamin' Jay Hawkins, who did his own freak-out cover version in 1973.

"Back in the USSR"

(John Lennon-Paul McCartney)

Artist: The Beatles

Year of Recording: 1968

Appears on: *The Beatles, 1967-1970*

Paul wrote "Back in the USSR" as a jokey acknowledgement that homesickness—even for a Cold War visitor to the United States from eastern Europe—is universal. The Beach Boys may have sung about "California Girls," but if you're from, say, Ukraine, you'll still default to your family ties and assume the ladies from your neighborhood are the best of the bunch.

The goofy satire couldn't prevent a testy recording session. Upon getting a lecture from Paul about how he'd botched a drum part, a fed-up Ringo Starr walked out and quit the band for a few days. Feeling unappreciated, he wallowed on comedian Peter Sellers's yacht and found the sea-set inspiration to compose "Octopus's Garden." Paul handled most of the beat until Ringo returned to the studio, where he found his kit covered remorsefully in flowers. A year later, after the Beatles performed on the rooftop of their London offices, Ringo received an unexpected and unsigned postcard from Paul, saying, "You are the greatest drummer in the world. Really."

"Pipes of Peace"

(Paul McCartney)

Artist: Paul McCartney

Year of Recording: 1982

Appears on: *Pipes of Peace, All the Best (*non-US version*) , Wingspan (Hits and History), Pure McCartney*

His solo career having regained both critical and popular footing with *Tug of War*, Paul used leftovers from those sessions for his follow-up and then obeyed a similar formula to fill any gaps. Like *Tug*, for example, *Pipes of Peace* kicks off with a plea for worldwide harmony and then cashes in on duets with one of the era's most bankable black-male vocalists. And in case the connection between the two projects wasn't obvious, the second side includes a mashup of the two title songs, presented as "Tug of Peace."

But *Pipes* weighs in a lot lighter than its predecessor. The shock of John Lennon's death, such an obvious approach to analyzing *Tug of War*, had lessened, and more of the music could at least attempt to be fun again (succeeding, I'd argue, a good half of the time). Instead

of making self-serious racial metaphors with Stevie
Wonder ("Ebony and Ivory" from *Tug*), Paul traded
lovesick lyrics over danceable rhythms with Michael
Jackson on "Say, Say, Say." Whereas Paul's call for
unity to start *Tug* was presented reverently to an
audience of adults, his updated slant on the same
message to kick off *Pipes* was bouncingly playful, as if
intended for the same impressionable children who
sing on it. He sounds more relaxed here in 1983 than
at any point in his post-Beatles career, maybe too much
so. Paul would pack stadiums beyond this point, but it
would be the last era in which he'd top the singles
charts in the United Kingdom on his own. The title
tune was a huge hit there, where fans of a certain age
still associate it with Christmas.

"Alligator"

(Paul McCartney)

Artist: Paul McCartney

Year of Recording: 2012 and 2013

Appears on: *New*

In 1979, the Guinness Book of Records hosted a
dinner for Paul and declared him the "Most Successful
Songwriter" and the "Most Honored Man in Music."
And why not? More than 130 of his songs have charted
in the United Kingdom, and in both the United States
and the U.K., at least 30 of those have hit the number-

one spot. That same person, though, is singing on "Alligator" about needing someone to lean on and claiming that everybody's doing better than him.

Are they just empty lyrics to surround a melody, or is the 71-year-old ex-Beatle feeling sadly unsatisfied here and believing he's still not living up to his own expectations? The accompanying album teamed Paul up with a set of hot, modern producers, including Mick Ronson (Amy Winehouse, Bruno Mars, etc.) and Paul Epworth (Adele, Florence + the Machine), perhaps to regain marketability with a younger audience. He'd also fallen in love again by then, to his third wife, Nancy Shevell. So, business aside, maybe even the ridiculously rich and famous view fresh romance as a mix of salvation and redemption. Or as Paul nearly puts it here, maybe every man is looking for someone to give his alligator to.

"Let 'Em In"

(Paul McCartney-Linda McCartney)

Artist: Wings

Year of Recording: 1976

Appears on: *Wings at the Speed of Sound, Wings Greatest, All the Best, Wingspan (Hits and History), Pure McCartney*

While still in the middle of promoting *Venus and Mars*, Paul took Wings back into the studio and made *At the*

Speed of Sound and timed its release to line up with the band's first concert tour of the United States. Either due to the rush or a simple desire to frame the group as a true team, it's the least Paul-centric entry in the band's discography. Denny Laine takes the lead on two songs, and all the other members (guitarist Jimmy McCulloch, the surprisingly soulful drummer Joe English and, yes, even Linda) get one featured track each. But the mostly weak tea is spiced up by two of Paul's biggest hits: the signature track "Silly Love Songs" and the opener, "Let 'Em In."

Before he met John Lennon and observed his friend's abandonment issues, Paul assumed everyone's family was like his own: Loyal, loving, and always up for a party with self-made music as the main entertainment. He pays tribute to some of his real relatives here, including his brother and his paternal aunt. The others referenced in the lyrics aren't actually tied to Paul by blood but receive just as much of a warm invitation to join the domestic festivities. Phil and Don, of course, are the revered Everly Brothers, Uncle Ernie is likely a nod to either Ringo Starr or Keith Moon, both of whom were close to Paul and played the Ernie character in different versions of the Who's rock opera *Tommy*. Sister Suzy, some have guessed, might be Linda. (She would put out a not-bad reggae single— "Seaside Woman"—under the pseudonym Suzy and the Red Stripes a year later.) Brother John, we can easily

211

assume, was Lennon, although Paul has said it might've been a subconscious choice.

The only inexplicable name is Martin Luther, who, it's usually believed, is MLK and not anyone connected to the Protestant Reformation. Since Paul never met either of those men, it must've been a case of the syllables and the melody just fitting well together.

"You Never Give Me Your Money"

(John Lennon-Paul McCartney)

Artist: The Beatles

Year of Recording: 1969

Appears on: *Abbey Road*

Seemingly always up for reuniting with John Lennon, Paul was nevertheless a no-show when he, George and Ringo were inducted into the Rock and Roll Hall of Fame in 1988. "It's unfortunate Paul's the one who's not here," George quipped at the podium, "because he's the one who had the speech in his pocket."

After breaking up in 1970, the Beatles were still forced to split their earnings four ways because of business entanglements. Paul asked to be freed from the arrangement, had his request denied due to alleged tax considerations for the others and sued his three friends. The band members remained in linked limbo until the most complex aspects of their partnership were finally dissolved in early 1975.

The 1975 legal split also meant each of the four needed to secure a new recording contract independently. The Beatles had been marketed by Capitol Records in America and by EMI in the rest of the world, and Paul was the only one who reupped with them rather than go elsewhere. By the time of the Hall of Fame ceremony, the other surviving members plus Yoko Ono had learned belatedly that as part of his revised deal with Capitol/EMI[78], Paul had been getting a larger cut of royalties on new sales of old Beatles albums than everyone else. The money had come out of the record company's share—not George's, Ringo's or John's—but the self-interested move reaggravated tensions and prompted the others to take legal action against Paul.

Instead of putting on a happy face at the ceremony, Paul stayed home and let the gathered guests perform "I Saw Her Standing There" without him. Three different giants of classic rock—Billy Joel, Bruce Springsteen and Mick Jagger—did Paul's vocal parts while Ringo and George played along.

---

[78] Paul signed different deals with Capitol/EMI in the mid-'70s and mid-'80s. There's debate as to which of those included the extra royalty. Mark Lewisohn told *Fabcast* it was the '70s contract.

"Sweet, Sweet Memories"

(Paul McCartney)

Artist: Paul McCartney

Year of Recording: 1991 and 1992

Appears on: No official album release (CD single only)

Following his two volumes of cheeky poetry, short stories and doodles in the 1960s, John Lennon was seen as the most literary of the Beatles. Paul waited until 2001 to publish his own book of lyrics and verse but had privately been putting pen to paper for non-songwriting purposes for years,

For *Off the Ground*, Paul ran all of his lyrics past poet Julian Mitchell. "Sweet, Sweet Memories," from those sessions, cruises along with an early-90s, rock-and-roll breeze during a time when his other creative output suggested an increasingly effusive love for wife Linda (see, for comparison, the equally obscure "Style, Style"). But most of the song's text actually comes from the 18th-century work "On a Certain Lady at Court" by Alexander Pope. Fans who like it, though, have generally needed to scour YouTube, eBay and other non-official channels to hear the track. Beyond inclusion as bonus material on a CD single, you can only find it on *Off the Ground: The Complete Works*, an expensive two-disc collection released exclusively in

Germany and the Netherlands. Given that Paul's people have a habit of compiling fancy "archive edition" box sets of his back catalog, here's hoping this era's rarities are next on the list.

"Penny Lane"

(John Lennon-Paul McCartney)

Artist: The Beatles

Year of Recording: 1966 and 1967

Appears on: *Magical Mystery Tour, 1967-1970, 1*

Only three years away from their bitter breakup, the Beatles were still incredibly close in 1967. Following a moped accident that left a scar on his upper lift, Paul was the first to grow a mustache, and the other three followed in solidarity as soon as their hair could grow. When John turned childhood memories into "Strawberry Fields Forever" as the first intended track for the *Sgt. Pepper* album, Paul polished off his own Liverpool-set reminiscences in the form of "Penny Lane[79]."

The differences between those two songs highlight the opposite upbringings of John and Paul. The boyhood

---

[79] Under pressure to put out new material, George Martin crossed "Strawberry Fields Forever" and "Penny Lane" off of *Sgt. Pepper* and let the band's record company put them out as a single instead.

abandonment that Lennon likely never got over might subconsciously explain the darkness in "Strawberry Fields," whereas the supportive domesticity that typified the McCartney house—even after Paul's mother's death—might account for the cheer in "Penny Lane[80]."

The contrast in those formative experiences fit well with each man's initial take on psychedelic drugs. In his search for escape from a painful past and an uneasiness toward fame, John claimed to have done acid nearly every day around this time, and his trippy state of mind hangs over all of "Strawberry Fields." Paul, though, was the last to dabble with LSD and didn't stick with it as long as his closest peer. "When acid came around," he said, "we'd heard that you're never the same…I think John was rather excited by that prospect. I was rather frightened by that prospect. I thought, 'Just what I need! Some funny little thing where I can never get back home again!'" And with a version of home as comfortably quaint as "Penny Lane" in his ears and in his eyes, who could blame him?

---

[80] The Beach Boys' *Pet Sounds* was another major influence on Paul at the time.

"Two of Us" (*Anthology* Version)

(John Lennon-Paul McCartney)

Artist: The Beatles

Year of Recording: 1969

Appears on: *Anthology 3*

The opener on the otherwise fairly tense *Let It Be*, "Two of Us" allowed Beatle fans to live in denial and pretend like everything between John and Paul remained warm and fuzzy. The duo harmonize together on the verses and chorus, and when Paul breaks away to sing the bridge—going on about long-lasting shared memories—even his solo feels like a big hug for his writing partner.

Paul burst a lot of bubbles when he admitted later that the song was more about his relationship with Linda and how she encouraged him to let go of stressors that were largely out of his control. The couple would get into a car at Linda's urging, and contrary to Paul's tendency toward order, ride around until they had no idea of where they were. As long as they were next to each other, the unknown could be an inviting destination.

For those who prefer it as a John/Paul love story, though, the version heard on the *Anthology* series doesn't disappoint. "Take it, Phil," Paul says to John around the midpoint, a reminder of their teenage bond over early rock-and-roll acts like the Everly Brothers.

"Cage"

(Paul McCartney)

Artist: Wings

Year of Recording: 1978 and 1980

Appears on: No official album release

Nothing if not prolific, Paul toyed with the idea of emptying his archive of unreleased songs several times. A pre-internet search for bootlegs might've unearthed multiple versions of an abandoned odds-and-sods compilation of stray tracks and non-album singles called *Hot Hitz and Kold Kutz*. The closest we got to an official release happened around 1979-1981, when Paul's enthusiasm for new work with Wings was at its lowest and while he coped with the doubled trauma of drug-related jailtime and John Lennon's murder. He'd signed a huge record deal with CBS, experienced fewer sales than expected and ultimately got pressure to give the guys in suits something for their big bucks besides quirky leftovers.

"Cage" remains locked away, another example of Paul's tendency to link multiple tunes into one. Recorded late in the band's career, the midsection about an apologetic boyfriend trying to walk it all back

218

nevertheless has the Paul/Linda/Denny Laine vocal blend of classic Wings.

"Jenny Wren"

(Paul McCartney)

Artist: Paul McCartney

Year of Recording: 2004

Appears on: *Chaos and Creation in the Backyard, Pure McCartney*

These days, Paul will tell you he wrote the Beatles classic "Blackbird" in response to the civil rights movement. People in his orbit at the time say it was inspired by a winged creature in nature, observed either during a mediation retreat in India or near the home of a relative. Other acts who covered the song (including Crosby, Stills and Nash, who played it as early as the Woodstock festival) claimed to have reframed it as a political metaphor long before Paul went public with his own explanation.

Less revisionist history has been alleged in regard to Paul's other "bird" tunes. There's "Bluebird" from *Band on the Run*, "Long Tailed Winter Bird" off *McCartney III* and "On the Wings of a Nightingale," which he gifted to his beloved Everly Brothers. My favorite among the flock had long been "Jenny Wren," until I learned that its name actually comes from a

Dickens character and not anything with wings. Like "Blackbird," though, the melody is inspired in part by a Bach piece. The mournful solo in the middle of the gentle lyrics is played on a duduk, an Armenian wind instrument.

"FourFiveSeconds"

(Paul McCartney-Kanye West-Kirby Lauryen-Mike Dean-Tyrone Griffin-Dave Longstreth-Dallas Austin-Elon Rutberg-Noah Goldstein)

Artist: Rihanna, Kanye West and Paul McCartney

Year of Recording: 2014

Appears on: No official album release (single only)

The Beatles recorded their first single, "Love Me Do," in September 1962. Until then, John Lennon had taken the main vocal on the song, but George Martin wanted John's harmonica in the arrangement as a hook, which couldn't be played live unless someone else manned the microphone. Paul was drafted and says he can still hear the nervousness in his own voice, his first time making a major record with his own band and suddenly having to take on more of the spotlight than expected.

Fast-forward 60 years or so, and it's possible that his last major successes on the radio (maybe?) will have been his "work" with Kanye West. The quotes are intentional there because Paul thought he was merely toying with some modest ideas while West rolled tape

220

and had no clue that any of it would amount to a song, let alone a major seller for Rihanna. When he first heard "FourFiveSeconds," he wasn't even sure he was on it. But then he realized his acoustic guitar groove had been sped up and used as the supportive spine for the whole track. How sped up, you ask? Well, can you hear the chipmunk voice underneath Mr. West's at just past the 50-second mark? That's Sir Paul McCartney, still making hits.

"Long Tailed Winter Bird"

(Paul McCartney)

Artist: Paul McCartney

Year of Recording: 2020

Appears on: *McCartney III*

While everyone else was on Zoom or baking bread, Paul spent the COVID lockdown making a new album almost completely by his isolated self.

McCartney III came out in late 2020 on streaming services, CD, cassette and 11 different versions of vinyl, each one in its own color. The point, it's supposed, was to entice collectors to buy the thing at least 11 times, thereby stacking the sales charts in Paul's favor. It sold 107,000 copies during its first week in the United States, not much compared to his 1970s catalog but with more seven-day vinyl purchases for any album in at least 25-plus years. It would've topped the main Billboard chart if not for Taylor Swift putting out new material at the same time. Her latest songs make it onto radio and have staying power in the sales rankings. His get gobbled up by loyal fans in their initial week, don't get played beyond a die-hard bubble and otherwise slip away quickly.

Commercial performance aside, *III* was the first of his self-titled, homemade trilogy to be embraced by his audience upon first listen instead of prompting bewildered shrugs. Maybe it's a byproduct of it having many more conventionally structured songs compared to the acoustic doodles of 1970's *McCartney* and the synthesizer exercises of 1980's *McCartney II*. Or maybe it's the result of Paul's transition to treasured-elder status. At this point, the people who adore him don't waste time picking apart problems with this track or that one. They just feel blessed to still have him around.

"Nineteen Hundred and Eighty-Five"

(Paul McCartney-Linda McCartney)

Artist: Wings

Year of Recording: 1973

Appears on: *Band on the Run, Pure McCartney*

"Kreen Akrore," "Power Cut," "Crossroads Theme," "Warm and Beautiful," "Baby's Request," "One of These Days," "Through Our Love," "Motor of Love," "Nod Your Head," "Road," "Hunt You Down."

If you're not familiar with those songs, you're not alone. When the Beatles put out albums, the track listing would be sequenced carefully with particular attention paid to an attention-getting opener and a barn-burning or eye-opening closer. "Twist and Shout," "Money," "Dizzy Miss Lizzie," "Tomorrow Never Knows," "A Day in the Life," "The End" and "Get Back" all got the last spot on a Beatles album and with good reason. Paul's solo and Wings output, despite all the sweet goodness in the middle of the cookie, tends to exit without much fanfare.

"Nineteen Hundred and Eighty-Five," which ends *Band on the Run*, is his most major exception. It's the rare last track that feels like a satisfying encore and an acknowledgement that the best albums take listeners

223

on a journey and leave people with a different feeling when the music stops than when it started.

Paul couldn't afford to be so casual in 1973, back when, out of all the Beatles (Ringo included), he had the lowest level of street credibility among serious rock fans. He needed *Band on the Run* to be huge in both its sound and its success, and it was. And just in case someone got near the final groove on the record having forgotten what had come before it, there's even a callback to the title song in the fadeout.

Always go out with a bang. Only a fool would do otherwise.

Acknowledgments

This project began as a series of posts on social media to a private group of longtime friends. For their encouragement, support and kindness, my gratitude goes out to Tom Shallcross, Anthony Rizzo and Chris Cali.

Much appreciation to Mohammad Gulam for his patience and help with the cover design.

Jonathan Hicks and Chris Ward have been the best friends my writing has ever had. Knowing both of them has been a professional and personal blessing.

A shoutout to Greg Rosensteel for driving me to various Chicagoland suburbs as part of our day jobs and cranking up Paul's greatest hits along the way.

Luka Jankovic made me believe I had something to share with the world, Paul-related and otherwise.

My father—Frank Styburski—spun *Revolver* again and again when I was merely four and thereby passed down a love for music.

Thanks to all.

Sources

Books.

The Beatles. *The Beatles Anthology*. San Francisco: Chronicle, 2000.

Brown, Craig. *150 Glimpses of the Beatles*. New York: Farrar, Strauss and Giroux, 2020.

Carlin, Peter Ames. *Paul McCartney: A Life*. New York: JR, 2009.

Coleman, Ray. *The Man Who Made the Beatles: An Intimate Biography of Brian Epstein*. New York: McGraw-Hill, 1989.

—. *McCartney: Yesterday & Today*. Los Angeles: Dove, 1996.

Costello, Elvis. *Unfaithful Music & Disappearing Ink*. Blue Rider Press, 2015

Davies, Hunter. *The Beatles*. New York: W.W. Norton, 2009.

Doyle, Tom. *Man on the Run: Paul McCartney in the 1970s*. New York: Ballantine, 2013.

Draper, Robert. *Rolling Stone Magazine: The Uncensored History*. New York: HarperPerennial, 1991.

Epstein, Brian. *A Cellarful of Noise*. London: Souvenir Press, 1964.

Gooden, Joe. *Riding So High: The Beatles and Drugs*. Pepper & Pearl, 2017.

Hagan, Joe. *Sticky Fingers: The Life and Times of Jann Wenner and Rolling Stone Magazine*. New York: Alfred A. Knopf, 2017.

Lewisohn, Mark. *The Beatles: Recording Sessions*. New York: Harmony, 1990.

—. *The Beatles: Tune In: (Extended Special Edition)*. London: Little Brown, 2013.

MacDonald, Ian. *Revolution in the Head: The Beatles' Records and the Sixties*. Chicago: Chicago Review Press, 2007.

Miles, Barry. *Paul McCartney: Many Years From Now*. New York: Owl, 1998.

Norman, Philip. *Paul McCartney: The Life*. New York: Back Bay, 2017.

Perasi, Luca. *Paul McCartney: Recording Sessions (1969-2013)*. Milan: L.I.L.Y., 2014.

Salewicz, Chris. *McCartney*. New York: St. Martin's, 1986.

Seaman, Frederic. *The Last Days of John Lennon*. New York: Birch Lane, 1991.

Sheff, David. *All We Are Saying.* Griffin, 2020.

Sheffield, Rob. *Dreaming the Beatles.* New York: Dey St., 2018.

Shotton, Pete and Nicholas Schaffner. *John Lennon: In My Life.* Stein & Day, 1983.

Sounes, Howard. *Fab: An Intimate Life of Paul McCartney.* Cambridge: Da Capo, 2011.

Spitz, Bob. *The Beatles: The Biography.* New York: Back Bay, 2005.

Weber, Erin Torkelson. *The Beatles and the Historians: An Analysis of Writings About the Fab Four.* Jefferson: McFarland, 2016.

Films

The Beatles Anthology (Expanded DVD Version). Directed by Geoff Wonfor. Apple, 2003.

The Beatles: The First U.S. Visit. Directed by Albert and David Maysles. Apple, 2004.

The Compleat Beatles. Directed by Patrick Montgomery. Metro-Goldwyn-Mayer/United Artists, 1984.

Give My Regards to Broad Street. Directed by Peter Webb. Twentieth Century Fox, 1984.

McCartney 3, 2, 1. Directed by Zachary Heinzerling. 2021.

Paul McCartney & Wings: Band on the Run. Directed by Mark Murray. ITV, 2010

Paul McCartney: Put It There. Directed by Geoff Wonfor. Picture Music International, 1989.

Wingspan. Directed by Alistair Donald. MPL, 2001.

Podcasts[81]

Alexanian, Ethan. *Fans on the Run*.

Carty, Jason and Steven Cockcroft. *Nothing Is Real*.

Edelson, Howie and Stephen Bard. *Fabcast*.

Erickson, Diana. *One Sweet Dream*. "The Making and Breaking of the Fab 4 Image."

Mercer, Chris and Ryan Brady. *Take It Away: The Complete Paul McCartney Podcast*.

Rodriguez, Robert (formerly with Richard Buskin). *Something About the Beatles*.

Shaw, Chris. *I Am the Eggpod*.

---

[81] Unless otherwise noted in quotation marks, research for this book included listening to all episodes of these programs up to June 6, 2021.

Things We Said Today[82]. "#184 - Author Philip Norman" and "#275 - Paul McCartney's Driving Rain."

Whiles, Sam. *Paul or Nothing.*

Wisbey, Joe. *Beatles Books.*

Websites

https://www.the-paulmccartney-project.com

---

[82] Many have hosted this show over the years, the one constant being Ken Michaels.